THE TAPAS LOV

MADRID

THE TAPAS LOVER'S GUIDE TO

MADRID

JO FERNANDEZ-CORUGEDO

WHITE OWL

AN IMPRINT OF PEN & SWORD BOOKS LTD.
YORKSHIRE – PHILADELPHIA

First published in Great Britain in 2025 by
White Owl
An imprint of
Pen & Sword Books Ltd.
Yorkshire - Philadelphia

ISBN 978 1 52679 205 1

A CIP catalogue record for this book is available from the
British Library.

Design: SJmagic DESIGN SERVICES, India.

The Publisher's authorised representative in the EU for product
safety is Authorised Rep Compliance Ltd., Ground Floor,
71 Lower Baggot Street, Dublin D02 P593, Ireland.
www.arccompliance.com.

For a complete list of Pen & Sword titles please contact

PEN & SWORD BOOKS LIMITED
George House, Beevor Street, Off Pontefract Road, Hoyle
Mill, Barnsley, South Yorkshire, England, S71 1HN.
E-mail: enquiries@pen-and-sword.co.uk
Website: www.pen-and-sword.co.uk

or

PEN AND SWORD BOOKS
1950 Lawrence Rd, Havertown, PA 19083, USA
E-mail: uspen-and-sword@casematepublishers.com
Website: www.penandswordbooks.com

MIX
Paper | Supporting
responsible forestry
FSC
www.fsc.org
FSC™ C016779

CONTENTS

INTRODUCTION

As my Spanish dad got older, if you asked what he wanted for his birthday he'd increasingly reply 'nothing', then when pushed he'd shrug and eventually agree on a bottle of hot pepper sauce or perhaps a piece of cheese. Although he didn't eat a huge amount, he loved food deeply and was regularly heard exclaiming: 'I live to eat, I don't eat to live.' Like a mantra. Because the handsome moustachioed Rafael Fernández-Corugedo was a total eccentric, he somehow got away with saying things that would be an irritating cliché if someone else did. And why pretend to want yet another pair of socks, a packet of pipe cleaners or pipe tobacco to mark another year passing when you could get something good to eat? So, something to eat, it always was. He will forever be associated with food in our family.

Dad was a truly great home cook, naturally creating tapas with his style of mainly small-scale Spanish dishes tailored to his diminutive appetite and stature. Born in Spain in 1927, statistically he was never going to be tall, or perhaps it was due to food shortage during the Spanish Civil War, but more of this later. And let's be honest, near constant smoking and drinking all his life – and he lived a fairly long life, until the age of 81 – was no doubt a dampener on his appetite. He probably could have run his own restaurant. He certainly could have built much of it and kitted out the interior after becoming a carpenter when he moved from London with

Dad photographed as a young man in Spain

my mum and oldest sister Megan to a village on the Essex/Suffolk borders. In his workshop, he created beautifully turned kitchens, lamps, tables, chairs, dressers and even, once, a doll for my sister Maria's birthday.

Despite being a heady mix of emotional, tactile, outgoing, loud and flirtatious – he was known to alternate between hugging and kissing you, breaking into song or tears – he didn't like to talk about his past much. It was more just the odd reminiscence here and there. It's a shame as so much history disappeared with him when he died, which was in many ways just as he lived, smoking a cigarette, in this instance lit from the gas hob in the kitchen. I think the past was just too painful for him. The time when your life should be full of fun and freedom – the teenage years – was traumatic and tough for him, coinciding with the Spanish Civil War, when he and his family suffered displacement, division, hunger and poverty along with millions of their fellow Spaniards. The 1936–39 war remains a scar on Spain's history, with mass systematic killings on battlefields and streets, torture, exiled Spaniards becoming refugees (many ending up in Nazi concentration camps) and families ruptured by the division in loyalty to Franco or the leftist Republicans.

Like his homeland, Dad swept all of this under the carpet for so many years. We don't know much about his history

before he met my mum, just snippets of conversations here and there. We know that his family was fairly middle class. That his dad was a Republican, defiant against General Franco's Fascist Nationalist army, ironically sheltered in Madrid, a Republican stronghold during the Civil War, by his Falangista (extreme Nationalist) sisters before he was eventually picked up on the street and sent to prison in Valencia. His family was sent to different parts of the country, presumably to find safety. On a rare moment of sharing the deeply packed-away ghosts of his past, Dad once opened up to me. He talked for a short while about how he used to carry cases for travellers arriving at the station to earn a few pesetas to buy food to feed his family, which included taking something to eat for his dad in prison. Some days all they had was a sweet potato. Perhaps this is another far sadder reason why he never ate more than he needed; just enough, but never too much. Aside from the odd open moment, if you wanted to ask him a question about anything in his life, you'd get nowhere, he'd sniff (he sniffed a lot), light his pipe and get back to watching the permanently turned-on television.

Conversely, growing up in the UK in the 1970s, our family of five wasn't rich, but we – my older sisters Maria, Megan and me – benefitted from his rich cultural heritage and grew up in easier political times. We'd take huge Spanish omelettes boxed up in a massive plastic Tupperware tub to the Essex coast on long, hot summer days out. My mum embraced Spanish food and drink both during and after their marriage, and in those days would have to take the train to Soho to buy chorizo or wait for his relatives to send turrón (a nougat-like sweet eaten at Christmas in Spain). This was before 'fancy foreign' food was available in supermarkets.

When he returned to Spain in his later years, settling in a little rural valley village in Alicante province with my younger sisters, Victoria and Cati, and stepmum Hilary, we older sisters would visit during the holidays. When his famous paella was ready to eat after he'd fussed over it for hours on the patio, we'd all crowd around the table as he declared it ready, greedy to get stuck in with our wooden forks and spoons. The gnarly rice which caught on the bottom of the metal paella pan was my favourite bit. His was hands-down the best paella I've ever tasted. Ever. He'd add chunky white butter beans for me, a not-so-strict vegetarian back then who didn't baulk at sharing the meat and fish-filled dish. His

rice was perfect, each grain separated from the other as it should – his mother taught him it should flick from a spoon to all sides of the table when ready – and despite the fact he's not around to make it anymore, it remains one of my top two favourite dishes in the world (the other is my ex-mother-in-law, Violet's, curry goat).

Dad proudly cooking a paella in his patio in Lliber, Alicante along with his son-in-law, Jon, and grandchild, Jonny

As you now know, Dad was a one-off. So, of course, there are a few more food-related Dad anecdotes to share. It should come as no surprise to learn he once filled our back garden with plastic buckets of snails, which he presumably got from some local river or coastal area. For some reason he neglected to do anything with them, so they just slithered around our back garden. My vegetarian future self would have been pleased with their survival. But our adventurous, global-eating and cooking mum was not, no doubt adding this to his growing catalogue of difficult-to-live-with eccentricities.

His love of gristly protein certainly annoyed more than one woman in our family. The stand-out food-related story was his insistence on cooking a pan of trotters for Victoria, then a teenager raising funds for the local village summer fiestas. As a festera, her role was to raise money for the following year's costumes. Embarrassed by the uncool pig-based dish, she begged him not to. He, of course, completely ignored her and insisted on cooking them, no doubt believing he was doing the right thing. He loved them and because he loved her it made sense (to him). It didn't end well. They exploded out of the pressure cooker, all over the kitchen, the sticky gelatin smears still visible on the ceiling where the pig's feet had hit the roof (just as my poor sister did...). A piece of trotter even ended up in her cousin's hair adding to several good reasons why this crazy day became known as el día de los patonets ('trotter day' in Valenciano, the official language of the Valencian Community).

In the early 1990s, I went to university in London to study Spanish (he somehow forgot to bring us up bilingual, resorting to odd words such as beso meaning kiss in English – nice enough but not enough). During the long summer holidays of my first year, I travelled around Spain with a student friend. Living on a grant, I remember the wide-eyed joy of receiving a free tapa with every drink we ordered, wondering why every country didn't follow suit, so that everyone who could afford a cheap beer or glass of wine got something to eat and soak up the booze.

These morsels of food, eaten with your fingers or a toothpick, served hot or cold, are still free with every drink in bars all over Spain. Granada is the best-known city for its generous free tapas, with dishes including refreshing salmorejo, crispy croquetas or pieces of fried fish. Wherever you are in Spain, from small portions of seafood to meat-filled pastries and slithers of cured meat, tapas represent an authentic, affordable way to sample local and national dishes. Some bars or restaurants pride themselves on their unique, comprehensive tapas menu while others stay loyal to that generous tradition of giving a simple, more traditional tapa with every drink.

Home to a winning combination of traditional and pioneering chefs and some of the best tapas in Spain, Madrid is one of the best places to sample this unique invention. Madrileños are justifiably obsessed with food, and tapas is an extension of this. The small word – and concept – is a disproportionately vast subject and represents how seriously it is taken here. Madrid has evolved into one of the richest culinary capitals of Europe, preserving its traditions while embracing creativity and innovation. It's worth noting how much the concept has been copied, with small plates featured on menus around the globe, even if they aren't referred to as tapas.

Tapas isn't just a culinary tradition, it's hugely cultural, as these small plates define and preserve the Iberian way of life. In a capital city that traditionally eats late, ordering a few tapas is a way to fend off hunger pangs until a dinner that's eaten quite a bit later than typically in the UK. It's also an incredibly sociable concept as you can share different dishes standing crammed in at a bar, trying to make eye contact with staff. For tourists, the grumpy barman who appears to ignore you can be off-putting but it's just the way it is; by contrast, white-jacketed older male waiters can often serve with charm, winks and a certain

style the majority of British people in the hospitality industry – myself included – don't achieve. Try not to take offence, once they serve you it's generally with some speed so they can move on to the next customer.

From classic tortilla de patatas (Spanish omelette) and jamón (ham) to calamares (fried squid rings) and caracoles (snails), tapas offer something for everyone. And remember, a few juicy olives, some slithers of sweet jamón and bread can combine to be tapas just as much as a slice of garlicky tortilla Española, (another name for Spanish omelette; don't worry there's a glossary in chapter one), a serving of ensaladilla Rusa (mayonnaise-drenched Russian potato salad) or a batch of fried green Padrón peppers (some hot, some not).

It's also worth noting that the tapas scene is steadily evolving. Years ago, vegan visitors would have had slim pickings in a traditional taberna, but now fully vegan tapas bars are popping up all over the city. I've devoted a chapter to both vegetarian and vegan tapas (see chapter seven).

This guide sets out to share where to find the best tapas in Madrid, from classic tabernas with the original smoke-stained ceramic tiling, creaky wooden barrels for tables and hams hung from above, to slick new dining spaces with concrete floors and Scandi-style furniture run by ambitious young chefs. It's not exhaustive – it couldn't possibly be. I'm including a selection in each major central area that I've tasted along with the family and friends who accompanied me.

A tapas tour of Madrid is the most pleasurable way to see the city's sights, landmarks and hidden streets, as you weave your way around during the day or immerse yourself in the energetic nightlife scene it's so famous for. You can choose an official company (see chapter nine) or treat it like a pub crawl. Pick an area with several tapas bars close together and move on to a new place after every drink and dish; unless a bar is so good you won't want to leave.

If Madrid is one thing, it's a city that knows how to live. As Dad loved to say, live to eat.

Also, like Dad, Madrid has a strong personality channelled through a combination of its long-standing food traditions, nightlife and a unique attitude to socialising. With thousands of places to eat tapas in Madrid, seeking out the best bars and restaurants can be overwhelming. This book isn't intended to be an exhaustive list of every tapas bar in the city, instead, it's a collection of tried and tested places from dusty old taverns dishing pig's ears and vermouth to five-star hotel bars doing fancy things with beetroot you'll be glad you tried.

TAPAS HISTORY, DEFINITIONS & GLOSSARY

If you grew up in the UK during the 1970s and the 1980s, as I did, the only accompaniment to a pint or glass of wine in a pub was a packet of crisps or peanuts, perhaps even a pickled egg, which, for some reason, was always placed inside the crisp packet, taken from a strange jar of brine on the bar that looked like it should be in a science lab. In contrast, the Spanish

Bar hopping in Madrid is the best way to sample tapas

had for centuries been enjoying a tradition of bars providing small amounts of homemade food to eat with their glass of wine or beer.

Tapas is something of a religion in Spain, woven into the fabric of society, and Madrid is the epicentre of it all. But before you disappear off into the city's mass of tapas bars and restaurants, hopefully with this book in hand, let's take a look at the origins of the Spanish tapa (the singular form of tapas). Some explanations for its creation are practical, others more mythical and possibly anecdotal: a bit more he-said, she-said or Spanish-whispers, if you like.

It's generally agreed that the concept originated in Andalucía, one of the most famous regions for tapas in Spain, although naturally, different regions all claim to be its birthplace.

One convenient, explanation concerns hygiene, and, as the story goes, a barman in a tavern serving a king, the name of the king in particular seems fluid, was aware of the flies buzzing around his glass of wine and placed a protective slice of ham on top. Tapar means to cover – and the word tapa means lid – so the notion of bar staff covering their customers' drinks with a slice of bread, ham or cheese to stop flies and dust from getting inside makes sense. Especially considering the temperatures Spain reaches in summer.

Then there's the one about King Alfonso X of Castile, who ruled during the thirteenth century – kings and the medieval era feature heavily in the reasons – who recovered from an illness by eating small amounts of food with his wine. After regaining his health, he decreed that all drinks should be served with a little something to eat on the side.

A similar story is that sailors and labourers would spend their salaries on alcohol rather than food, getting drunk and rowdy in the process. In order to clamp down on this, the then King, Felipe III, passed a law that every goblet of alcohol must be served with a plate of food included in the price (so this could also be the birth of free tapas). Another theory focuses on the rural workers whose long working hours and labour-intensive days meant they needed a glass of wine with a small snack, in between their lunch and dinner.

Another reason thrown into the ring is that in the traditional taverns drinkers stood at the bar, something that still happens today, and they'd place a small plate on top of their drink. Then again, some say in Andalucia the salty cured meats used to keep flies out of drinks made drinkers thirsty – in the same way crisps and peanuts do today – and as bar owners realised this, so they increased the practice. The south of Spain serves more free tapas with every drink order than in other places, so there may be some logic to this theory.

In reality, how can we know if there's one definitive reason? Perhaps the truth lies in a mishmash of all the above. What we do know is that regardless of how they developed, the origins of tapas are very much entwined with Spain's history. The Romans came and planted various grains, olive trees and grape vines, and the Arabs arrived armed with citrus fruits, almonds and spices, which all appear in tapas eaten around Spain, each region having its own speciality. These ingredients did and do form the basis of traditional tapas, using a few simple elements such as vegetables, cheese, meat and fish.

What's set in stone is that Madrid's culture is all about going out for tapas – ir de tapas, as the Spanish say – in bars and restaurants ranging from deeply traditional to modern, trying out different dishes.

Tapas in Madrid

What is served as tapas varies according to region but in general it is a mouthful of something simple, practical and cheap. Madrid's local specialities are patatas bravas (spicy fried potatoes), Spanish omelette, croquettes, aged cheese, squid sandwiches, ham and offal dishes. Often the tapas are laid out on the counter so you can see what's available.

Madrid is home to some of the best tapas bars in Spain (Insider Tours)

There is a unique quality to Madrid's bars and restaurants, whether they are a hundred years old or newer and conceptual, which stems from being rooted in Spanish culture and produce. The food scene here keeps on changing, but there's loyalty; bars selling home-style dishes remain popular yet there's room for venues merging traditional Spanish dishes with contemporary and fusion-style.

Madrid's tapas culture is also influenced by the weather, which means cooling off with chilled gazpacho (tomato soup) in summer or warming up with cocido madrileño (a rich stew) in winter. While there are tapas bars to suit all budgets and occasions, the best tapas bars in Madrid rest on the quality of their dishes, regardless of service or style.

In Madrid, Casa Labra, Bodega La Ardosa and La Casa del Abuelo are well-known places to sample some traditional Madrid-style tapas. Most of them have been open for over a hundred years and are highly regarded.

Free Tapas

One of the greatest traditions in Spain is the generous concept of the free tapa with every drink you order. Although not every city, town or village does this, and what you get can differ wildly from place to place. Lots of bars will immediately give you tiny bowls of olives, peanuts or chorizo slices when you order a glass of wine or beer. These are not to be confused with tapas, pinchos or raciones, which also can come free, although it is easy to.

This book will highlight bars that offer free tapas with the olive symbol and examples of what to expect.

Tapas, Raciones & Pinchos (Pintxos)

So now we've tossed about a few theories around the birth of tapas and what they are, let's get familiar with the terms used to describe the tapas you'll find in bars and restaurants and the descriptions of dishes.

Tapas

Pretty much any traditional dish can be served in a small portion with a drink, so you can find tapas consisting of paella (a rice dish from Valencia), migas (fried breadcrumbs), bacalao (cod), salmorejo (chilled tomato, bread and garlic soup), and much more. There are free tapas and those you pay for.

Raciones

Essentially sharing plates, a concept found throughout the Mediterranean, the ración – meaning portion in Spanish – is a larger serving of tapas. You'll also see media ración (half portion) on menus and blackboards outside bars.

Pinchos/Pintxos in Basque – Small bites on Bread

Essentially, these are tapas placed on slices of baguette – sometimes with toothpicks sticking out of them and can have almost anything on them, such as tortilla, Russian salad or simply a slice of Manchego cheese or jamón. Or they can be a bit more exciting with poached eggs, eels, anchovies, roasted peppers. You'll find pintxos all around Spain, but it's undisputed that the best pintxos in the country come from the north, particularly in San Sebastian.

Encurtidos – Pickled Foods

These include olives, gherkins, aubergines and spring onions preserved in a vinegar and salt solution, ensuring that they retain all their flavour. They are then served as appetisers and often found stuffed with anchovies or peppers.

Montaditos – Open Sandwiches

The word sandwich doesn't really explain montaditos, which are generally made with sliced baguette-style bread and can be topped with anything from chorizo to jamón, cheese, pickled vegetables, anchovies and other seafood.

Tapas Traditions

Order a few dishes at a time, rather than all at once. It's usual to order two or three tapas plates every 30 minutes or so, so you space them out and have one or two with every drink.

Eat tapas with your hands. Most dishes are designed to be picked up and put in your mouth easily (or with a toothpick).

TAPAS TALK, A GLOSSARY, FROM A–Z

Aceitunas – Olives

An essential tapas ingredient, Spain has such a variety of olives, both green and black, from the giant gordal olives of Seville to the smaller manzanilla. Some are briny, some swimming in oil, but all are perfect with a cold drink.

Albóndigas – Meatballs

Meatballs aren't particular to Spain, but the Spanish take is incredibly well done. Full of garlic, parsley and other spices, albóndigas are soft and easy to eat – a good-for-you fast food, if you like. Served with a seemingly endless supply of bread, which you can dip in the tomato sauce, a couple can make a meal by themselves.

Alcachofas – Artichokes

One of the best dishes involving artichokes is a la plancha, meaning grilled (on a hot plate) when the artichokes have been smashed and the tips of the leaves are char-grilled and gnarly.

Alioli – Oil & Garlic Sauce

A simple yet punchy oil and garlic sauce made by pounding garlic into a paste and then gradually adding olive oil, goes with almost any dish. Sometimes called aioli.

Banderillas – Small Skewers

Easy-to-eat ingredients often from a jar such as olives, anchovies and pickled red peppers speared together.

Berenjenas con Miel – Aubergine with Honey

A classic Andalusian tapas dish: fried slices of aubergine with honey drizzled over for a delicious combination of sweet and savoury.

Bocata / Bocadillo de Calamares – Squid Sandwich

Golden squid rings deep fried in olive oil encased in a crusty bread roll and topped with a dollop of alioli or a squeeze of lemon are a classic Madrid tapa. It's a cheap and cheerful snack to be eaten at any time. Eat it standing up for authenticity.

Boquerones – Anchovies

Spain has around 8,000 kilometres of coastline – landlocked Madrid, not so much. However, fish is usually among

Boquerones (anchovies) are a popular tapa in land-locked Madrid

the top of the tapas menu. Silver anchovies en vinagre – marinated in vinegar or olive oil – are perfect to pick at.

Buñuelos de Bacalao – Cod Fritters
Deep-fried salt cod fritters are made with a combination of flour, eggs, milk or water and butter, and they are usually flavoured with fresh parsley, salt, and pepper. Similar are tajadas de bacalao, usually slices of cod fried until golden brown and crispy, served with a squeeze of lemon.

Callos – Tripe and other Offal
Pretty much ubiquitous in most Madrid bars, callos a la Madrileña are Madrid's take on the traditional stew, served in a clay dish, along with slices of chorizo, blood sausage and ham.

Casquería – Offal
Traditionally used in Madrid home cooking, now offal is being creatively reinvented in contemporary menus but will always be on old-school tapas menus, along with pork cheek, tripe and trotters. Yes, they are an acquired taste – you either like them or you don't.

Champiñones – Mushrooms
Spaniards stuff the humble mushroom with chorizo cubes or herbs and lemon juice, grill it and elevate it into something a bit more interesting and smoky tasting.

Chopitos – Baby Squid
Deep-fried baby squid lightly battered and fried in olive oil.

Chorizo – Pork Sausage
This is a cured sausage blending chopped pork meat and fat seasoned with paprika and sometimes garlic.

Chorizo a la Sidra – Chorizo with Cider
This simple tapa is basically coin-sized slices of chorizo boiled in good cider, until it forms a syrup.

Croquetas – Croquettes
Deep fried cylinders of bechamel sauce coated in breadcrumbs, croquetas tend to be of the jamón variety although they can be filled with anything.

Ensalada Rusa – Russian Salad
Also known as ensaladilla Rusa or sometimes just ensaladilla, this is one of the most classic tapas dishes made from potatoes, peas, carrots and tinned tuna mixed with mayonnaise. It's not something that uses fresh ingredients, more store-cupboard staples, as you could pretty much assemble it from tins, so in that way it's the opposite of the good quality slices of jamón or cheese that form the tapas base. Spanish chef José Andrés changed the traditional name to Ensaladilla Ucraniana on all of his menus in solidarity with the people of Ukraine.

Gambas – Prawns

Gambas al ajillo are prawns sautéed in a garlic oil, usually topped off with lemon and served in a rustic earthenware bowl. When the prawns are gone, use a few slices of bread to mop up the leftover garlic-infused oil. The tradition began in 1939 at the end of the Spanish Civil War when basics such as bread were hard to get hold of yet small prawns were readily available.

Gazpacho – Cold Tomato Soup

If you've experienced Spain in summer, you'll understand the magic of this cold soup made from tomato, cucumber, bell pepper, onion and garlic. It is often served in a glass, which means you can see the lovely red colour (not to be confused with salmorejo, see below).

Gildas – Basque Skewers

Briny olives, salty anchovies and spicy-ish long yellow-green pickled guindilla chilli peppers (also called piparras).

Huevos Estrellados – Bashed Eggs

The literal translation isn't perfect – these are something between fried and scrambled eggs, broken up and served on hot, hand-cut chips.

Huevos Rotos – Broken Eggs (sometimes called estrellados)

This very simple dish is found in many of Madrid's bars and taverns and it's

Gambas al ajillo (Insider Tours)

Gildas are made with anchovies, olives and peppers (Insider Tours)

something you could easily make at home: chips and jamón topped with loosely fried eggs. The huevos rotos served at Casa Lucio (Cava Baja, 35) are legendary.

Jamón Ibérico – Iberian Ham
Cured Iberian ham is a typically Spanish food. The difference between jamón Ibérico and jamón serrano is that the meat of the former comes from free-range Iberian pigs raised in the meadows of Extremadura and Andalusia, on a diet consisting essentially of acorns. Jamón de Recebo is made from a cross between jamón Ibérico de Bellota and jamón serrano and is generally less expensive than either, with a shorter curing time. The flavour is intense, and the fat content is less. Jamón Iberico de Cebo is made from acorn-fed pork and has a higher fat content and is also less expensive.

Cured Iberian ham is a typical tapas (Insider Tours)

Judías Viudas – Widow Beans
If you've overdone the chorizo or are vegetarian or vegan, you'll enjoy this warming, comforting concoction of pinto beans, tomato, onion, carrot, pepper, extra virgin olive oil, sea salt, garlic and spices. Although look out, as any Spanish dish like this can sneak in some chorizo.

Migas de Pan – Breadcrumbs
The definition of cheap and cheerful, like some of the best dishes, was created by peasants and shepherds to

use up stale bread. Torn up bread, olive oil, salt, pepper, garlic with bits of meat such as chorizo are added to it.

Mojama – Salt-Cured Tuna
Popular in Spanish cuisine, this filleted tuna served in wafer-thin slices adds a salty flavour to dishes.

Navajas – Razor Clams
These sweet, delicate seafood pieces are often served grilled with a fresh-tasting dressing of garlic, olive oil and parsley.

Patatas con Alioli – Potato Salad with Alioli
This ubiquitous Spanish tapas and side dish mixes soft boiled potatoes wrapped in the classic Mediterranean thick and creamy garlic sauce.

Patatas Bravas – Spicy Potatoes
Uncomplicated and filling, this dish is basically fried potato chunks smothered in sauce. The sauces are what elevates them, with garlicky alioli or brava, an orange-brown spicy, tomato sauce. Sometimes you might even get a little bit of both drizzled on top. Perfect for sharing.

Picos – Bite-sized Breadsticks
These teeth-breakingly crunchy breadsticks made from bringing together flour, olive oil, yeast and salt are a staple of any Spanish bar, served with cheese and charcuterie.

Pimientos de Padrón – Padrón Peppers
These smallish Spanish peppers are a good-looking shade of dark green and tend to be fried in olive oil then showered with ridiculous amounts of rock salt. In every batch, a few peppers are hot, and the rest are not – you never know until you try one. Think of it as Russian roulette for the tastebuds.

Pisto – Vegetable Stew
If overloading on potatoes, bread and ham have you yearning for some healthy vegetables, order this richly-coloured ratatouille-like tomato-based stew with caramelised onions, and vegetables such as aubergines and courgettes in olive oil, usually served as a side.

Pulpo a la Gallega – Galician Octopus
All the way from Galicia, this is boiled octopus seasoned with olive oil, salt, and a good sprinkle of paprika.

Queso Manchego – Manchego Cheese
This hard salty cheese pairs perfectly with bread and some jamón Iberico or serrano and a glass of Ribera red wine. It's great for first timers because the cheese does not have a particularly strong taste and it's also something that you will find on nearly every menu across Spain.

Salmorejo – Cold Soup
This typical southern dish from Andalusia is thicker and richer

Salmorejo cold tomato soup (Insider Tours)

than gazpacho and doesn't contain cucumber or peppers, but a bit of bread, garlic and, of course, great tomatoes. The colour is orange and it tends to be garnished with hard-boiled eggs, diced serrano ham and a drizzle of olive oil.

Salpicón de Marisco – Seafood Salad

A fresh and prettily presented summer dish of prawns, mussels and octopus, dressed with vinaigrette.

Sobrasada – Soft Chorizo

A soft cured sausage made from pork meat with a spreadable texture, originating in the Balearic Islands.

Tomates Aliñados – Seasoned Tomatoes

This dish rests with the fresh slices of sun-ripened tomatoes Spain excels in dressed with a vinaigrette of extra virgin olive oil, salt, pepper and vinegar.

Tortilla Española – Spanish Omelette

Also known as tortilla de patatas – potato omelette – this humble dish might be the most common tapa out there. Softened potato pieces mixed with egg then fried into a pleasing cake-like shape can be eaten hot or cold. In Madrid the eggy centre is mainly runny; if that's not your bag, accept that's just the way it is, avoid it or work your way around the outside. Some add onion, some don't. Another hot topic to discuss late into the night.

Torreznos – Pork Crackling
Fried pieces of salty pork belly with a crispy crackling-style top.

Zamburiñas – Scallops
Yes, there is a tapa starting with 'z'. These small scallops served in a half shell are typical fresh seafood tapas.

Should you need to order a drink or two...
  'Una cerveza, por favor' gets you a beer but you need to be more specific in Spain in terms of quantity.

Una Caña – a small glass of draft beer, a little less than a half pint.

Un Doble – yes, twice as much as a caña, which some bars don't offer.

Chupitos – shots of aromatic liqueurs.

Un Vermut / Vermú – vermouth is an aromatic drink beloved of Madrileños served with a slice of orange, revered at the 'hora de vermut'. Some bars serve it de grifo (on tap).

Un Vaso de Agua/una Botella de Agua – a glass or bottle of water is needed for so much salty food and by law all venues provide tap water.

2

CHAMBERÍ, SALAMANCA & RETIRO

Just north of Parque del Buen Retiro, more of which later, Chamberí is a heady combination of elements, at once posh, traditional, residential and therefore largely tourist-free. Created as a lovely place for haughty Spanish aristocrats to live, today it's known for the eye-wateringly expensive property and flowing lines of the art nouveau mansions along the wide streets (a feature that's always the sign of a fancy district). As you hop from bar to bar, be sure to peek through any open doors into high-ceilinged hallways revealing well-turned staircases lit with vintage chandeliers on streets where the boutique shop windows display the expensive crockery and smart children's clothes to suit the local pockets.

Yet Chamberí is a district that is also cultural and feels authentically Madrid. You probably won't find landmarks in tourist guides such as the La Casa de Las Flores, a boxy 1930s brick apartment block where Chilean poet Pablo Neruda took up residence after arriving here in the mid-1930s. He even mentioned the Casa de Las Flores in some of his well-known poems. Named for the flower-fringed balconies and terraces – flores means flowers in Spanish – that embellish the apartments on the corner of Calle de la Princesa, it was designated a historical landmark as an example of early modernist architecture. Come from the direction of the Plaza de Colón and you can't miss Julia, a massive 12-metre high white-resin sculpture of a woman's head, eyes closed in contemplation, created by Catalan public artist Jaume Plensa.

Famed for his depictions of the human face, Plensa designed the sculpture to take the attention off the also-white marble monument to the square's no longer revered namesake, Cristobal Colón (Christopher Columbus in English). Here also, the Mercado de Vallehermoso retains its old school vibe, avoiding being pimped into a fancier, less authentic venue as happens to many.

Over a decade ago, Calle Ponzano became the place to go for tapas and nightlife in Madrid and even spawned

Julia, a sculpture by Jaume Plensa, in Plaza de Colón

its own hashtag #Ponzaning and website (ponzaning.es). It's still a long stretch of street where some of the city's best bars and restaurants are to be found. Here among the residential blocks and bars, Plaza de Olavide is a circular-shaped pedestrianised square with something for everyone – parents can sit, possibly sipping a beer at one of the many bars and restaurants that encircle it, and watch their kids run around the grassy, well-planted green space and cooling fountain, or jumping all over the multiple playgrounds.

It's all about terrace culture, sitting outside during the warmer months, soaking up a fine bit of urban planning. Malasaña became one of the most spirited places for going out; however, now one of the most traditional areas of Madrid, it is becoming a lot more interesting in terms of nightlife.

Perhaps even posher than Retiro, and designed in the late nineteenth century as an exclusive enclave for the Spanish aristocracy, Salamanca is distinguished by its grid-like boulevards, glamorous shops and well-stocked galleries, from where some of the private collections owned by aristocrats and bourgeois were first made available to the public after the civil war. The Golden Mile is a network of streets thick with designer boutiques for those with money to burn, from Hermès to Versace, Chanel, Louis Vuitton and Jimmy Choo. Shoppers rest up in the tapas bars that add character to the barrio. A former cinema, close to Plaza de Colón, Platea is Madrid's most up-market market, blurring the lines between food and theatre with a red-curtained stage for shows and balconies perfect for people-watching. Not forgetting the food, which among the big-name chef Michelin-starred restaurants includes El Patio, a designated tapas area with table service so you don't miss the show.

You don't need to pass through one of Madrid's museums to see work by famous Spanish artists. At the end of Avenida de Felipe II, Plaza de Salvador Dalí features Salvador Dalí's tribute to Isaac Newton, a bronze sculpture figure of the gravity man himself. Since its 1980s inception, the granite-slabbed square has been landscaped by a modern architect, adding trapezoid-

The boating lake at Parque del Buen Retiro, which gives its name to the refined area (photo by Sara Riaño, Unsplash)

shaped wooden planters with benches on one side designed to allow shade as the city hots up.

Unesco-protected Retiro borders Salamanca and is named after the Parque del Buen Retiro, once an exclusive enclave reserved for Spanish royalty and the aristocracy, until it was opened to the public at the end of the nineteenth century. Now it's all things to everyone: children run around decoratively curved fountains and towering statues such as Ángel Caído (Fallen Angel), which depicts Lucifer's fall from the heavens, apparently placed at 666 metres above sea level; locals jog, walk city-sized small dogs (some are visible in dog prams) and sip coffee in open-air cafes overlooking the green lake. You could spend a day here in the La Rosaleda rose garden where over 4,000 bloom each May by the fisherman's cottage, and the glassy Palacio de Cristal, a copy of Crystal Palace in south London. Here also is ahuehuete, a centuries-old tree taken from South America during Colonialism, and a wood of 192 olive trees and cypresses planted to mourn those who died in the 2004 bombing at nearby Atocha station. Despite rubbing shoulders with the Prado Museum, part of the 'big three' along with the Reina Sofia and the Thyssen-Bornemisza, there's a down-to-earth feel to this neighbourhood that's largely residential but sneaks in pockets of shops and restaurants full of locals –

and non-locals – sampling authentic Spanish cuisine.

Read on for a selection of places to eat for tapas lovers.

La Barra del Gourmet, El Corte Inglés

If you're seeking a more serene experience, glide down the escalator to the glamorous basement restaurant of the Spanish retail institution, El Corte Inglés' glass-fronted Salamanca store. In the Gourmet Club grocery area, join the well-dressed locals in their smart summer uniform of crisp white jeans, wedge espadrilles and lots of gold jewellery. Staff sport equally smart navy blazers and braces. Among the luxurious surroundings with blonde herringbone parquet floors, a marble bar and clutches of tables of La Barra del Gourmet, there's a lot to choose from on a menu that spans oysters to charcuterie, gildas to empanadas. If you need something fresh, try a crispy salad, livened up with tuna, tomato, onion, artichoke and red pepper served on beautiful crockery. You will be surrounded by the expensive bottles of olive oil, hams, cheeses, tins of tuna, jars of anchovies and other goodies that adorn the shelves. Many of the El Corte Inglés stores are places for shopping and fine dining – in the gourmet area of the Castellana store, you can eat Michelin-starred dishes whizzed up by revered Spanish chef Dabiz Muñoz; upstairs in this branch Street XO turns a section of the third floor into a full-on Asian-fusion street food fest.

Calle de Serrano, 47, 28001, elcorteingles.es

Street XO

Staying in El Corte Inglés in Salamanca, the sister to Diver XO, Madrid's only three-Michelin-starred restaurant, Street XO makes a noise (visually and volume-wise) on the third floor of Madrid's main department store. How much the Spanish revere El Corte Inglés, a bit like our John Lewis, is revealed by the fact that the Castellana branch became the first department store in the world to be awarded a Michelin star thanks to chef Dabiz Muñoz's Ravio XO restaurant. The youngest chef in Spain to gain three Michelin stars by the age of 33 (he's currently in receipt of four), he launched Street XO as a conceptual kind of place with a street food menu. The restaurant's menu and interior are inspired by Asian street food stalls, with chefs preparing multi-layered

Fusion food at StreetXO

dishes in front of hungry customers. Stools line the long red bar where you can watch fusion tapas dishes whipped up in the open kitchen. Expect flavour combinations such as croquetas de la pedroche, with kimchi, sheep's milk, tuna sashimi and Lapsang Souchong tea and crispy pig's ear with strawberry hoisin sauce, aioli and pickle slices. The Tako de Pulpo is a tiny arrangement of grilled Galician octopus on a blue taco with fine shavings of parmesan cheese covering a combo of tamarillo emulsion, pickled carrots, and pumpkin seeds.

Calle de Serrano, 47, 28001, streetxo.com

Entre Cáceres y Badajoz

Every round of drinks – even a humble glass of cold tap water – comes with a free tapa at this no-frills corner barrio bar, slightly off the tourist trail, on the edge of Salamanca. Here, bullfighting is a firm, if controversial, theme: a side room has a glassy-eyed bull's head mounted on the wall and framed bullfighters' photos hang all over the place. Not surprisingly, it's pretty close to the Colosseum-like Las Ventas bullring, the largest in Spain that's sadly still in use. If the bullfighting paraphernalia upsets you, turn your back on it and get ready to eat sitting on the stools tucked around the decorative wooden barrels used as tables that frame the half-

tiled space or the long bar overhung with garlic and the obligatory legs of jamón. Join the masses who come to tuck into generous amounts of tortillitas de camarones, tasty prawn fritters made from a combination of a few basics – chickpea flour, onion and parsley – which the chef turns into something incredible; tuna empanadas (turnovers) or good old tortilla de patatas. It's a local favourite for the high-quality homestyle cooking and packs out at weekends, so get there ahead of your hunger – and the crowds.

Calle de Don Ramón de la Cruz, 109, 28001.

Bar Tomate

Part of Barcelona-based Grupo Tragaluz with a spreading collection of restaurants in Mallorca, on the Costa Brava and three more in Madrid, Bar Tomate stands out as a contemporary neighbourhood spot in Chamberí, on the borders of Salamanca, an area home to embassies and the mansions of those who work in them. You'll spot it by the out-of-place sturdy-looking industrial-style benches and tables outside on the terrace; inside walls have been given a soft coat of grey paint, wooden floorboards are fuss free and handsome waiters wear man buns. It's an all-day kind of place, from coffee in the morning to tapas lunches and dinners.

Bar Tomate is a relaxed neighbourhood spot in Chamberí

There's also a wood-fired oven, which produces perfectly topped roasted pizzas, which draw diners along with the tapas selection. Tapas dishes can sometimes be a bit beige – potato, bread, mayonnaise and so on – but the menu here is full of inventive combinations delivered on beautiful ceramic plates such as spinach and ricotta croquettes with the surprising addition of pine nuts and a gorgeous green filling – creamy not sticky – inside the crispy coating. Fusion dishes include fried aubergine,

a classic tapa, here given an Asian-style twist with a sticky brown sauce of honey and orange, topped with sesame seeds. The same creative touch was given to corvina ceviche, slithers of raw fish with salmorejo, smokey with a hint of heat from the rocoto chilli and creamy avocado. If you turn up and there's no tables free, you'll still find standing room at the bar, where it's often most fun.

Fernando El Santo 26, 28046, grupotragaluz.com

Lamucca de Almagro

This chain of 13 or so Madrid restaurants with a conscience – the website regularly updates exactly how many Euros they've donated to social projects so far – means you can justify your night out in any one of them. Just off the Plaza de Alonso Martinez – and the Metro station of the same name – the Chamberí branch is an appealing space with the right design pieces to create a bistro feel: bare brick walls, low metal lamps, long mirrors (either designed so that diners can see themselves eat or to create a feeling of space) and studded banquette seating lining one wall and bentwood chairs face the restaurant side of long tables.

On a Monday night, it's filling up by 9pm with groups celebrating birthdays, families with tiny babies in buggies and solo diners. The young team bring tapas dishes such as croquettes in a silver basket on faux newspaper with Trump's favourite 'fake news,' in English, fresh from the fryer, golden crispy panko crumbs holding the inside that's studded with flecks of jamón. Other tapas dishes include Padrón peppers and slow cooked artichokes with crispy ham. If you're tired or lazy and staying in one of the area's too comfortable hotels you could order a takeaway (but you'd miss the charm).

Calle Almagro 3, 28010, lamuccacompany.com

Lamucca de Almagro has a varied menu including classic tapas dishes

Los Torreznos

Just as crispy, salty crackling is loved as a pub snack or roast pork is for a Sunday lunch in the UK, so torreznos are beloved by Spaniards. Strips of skin-on bacon fried or grilled to a crisped perfection are a guilty pleasure of many. If you're going to try this tasty little snack, then a place called Los Torreznos bodes well. Try them on their own or chopped up into smaller pieces and encased in tacos mixed with oh-so-pretty pico de gallo (chopped tomato, onion, serrano peppers with coriander) and drenched in thick wedges of fresh lemon. The Chamberi restaurant – one of three in the city stretching back to 1957 – is decked out like a smarter version of a fast-food chain in terms of decor. It's bright and light-filled (there's no soft lighting for those hiding their porky guilty pleasure), marble-topped tables and swift service. Free tapas appear in the form of montaditos topped with slim slices of perfectly cooked Spanish omelette sat on a slice of tomato and another with an oval slice of ruby-coloured chorizo, also with tomato and cheese. The pig connection is fully emphasised, from the hams hanging in the window to the imprinted pig shapes on the plastered walls.

Calle Alonso Cano 69, 28003, lostorreznosbar.es

Torreznos is known for its authentic atmosphere and crispy pork tapas

Torreznos

Taberna El Madrileño

Locals come regularly to this relative newcomer, a couple of blocks from the Plaza de Olavide in Chamberí for the good value menú del día, which provides three courses of home-style dishes and a drink. The starter includes satisfying salmorejo, which you can also order as a tapas dish on its own, along with a host of other typical tapas such as Russian salad, anchovies and squid. Served in a generously sized 1980s-style square white bowl, this is the perfect summer dish. Cold, creamy and that perfect pinky-red sunset shade, with added protein and a contrast in texture from the boiled egg yolk and crispy ham garnish on top. It's served with a chunky slice of white baguette to dip in or mop up the residue on the bottom of the bowl. Sit outside on the white plastic tables and chairs set under large parasols or step inside where faux plants trail over the bar

Above and below: *Taberna El Madrileño dishes smooth salmorejo*

area. Service is speedy – if you were in a hurry with just time for one tapa you could be in and out in under 30 minutes.

Calle de Eloy Gonzalo 20, 28010.

Hermanos Vinagre

Named for the pickled elements so beloved of Spanish tapas dishes, this small but growing chain of Madrid-based restaurants includes a slender bar on a corner street in Chamberí. Specialising in cocktails and small plates, the chef-patron Valentí brothers wanted to create a shiny new version of a traditional tapas bar, with high quality ingredients they had quite a hand in turning into riffs on classics. The pair pickle and smoke their mussels and anchovies (the latter hailing all the way from the green-clad lands of Cantabria in the north), for example, to provide the classic tapas such as anchovies in vinegar (the logo is a happy seeming anchovy wearing a hat...) or gildas (mini skewers). Non-brine-based dishes include made-to-order croquettes with hard boiled eggs hidden inside the bechamel sauce. The look is simple, but it works – a cheerful red and white diner-like theme with a stainless-steel bar and mosaic floor. Dogs are welcome, which works well for diners eating out in a city where every other person seems to have a small dog on a lead, in a pram or in

Hermanos Vinagre specialises in cocktails and small Plates

their arms when the pavement is too hot for their paws.

Calle del Cardenal Cisneros 26, 28010, hermanosvinagre.com

Sylkar

'How do you like your eggs in the morning?' goes the Dean Martin song. In Spain, the question is, how do you like your eggs in your tortilla de patatas? If you like your eggs runny, be sure to try the award-winning tortilla on the menu at Sylkar. The owners have yet to change their tortilla recipe since opening in 1970, winning numerous contests and up there with some of the best places to eat this simple dish in the city (the window humbly displays faded press cuttings detailing their fame). It's a tiny, unassuming place on one of Chamberí's wide side streets, a couple of blocks from Alonso Cano metro, with a dining room upstairs. For a ring-side seat where tapas are concerned, sit at the street-level bar with the locals who breeze in and out for pinchos and cañas while nosing at the goodies under the glass counter, from sauce-coated meatballs to a less sickly-looking Russian salad than other bars serve, this one with olives, and anchovies in oil. The service is prompt and, for once, an all-female team.

Order a drink and a little saucer of baguette slice and pork in a rich tomato sauce is proffered. In summer it's got to be pinky-orange gazpacho, this one thicker than some and rich in olive oil. Behind the bar, a large marble board holds all the essentials for a tapas bar – a baguette and giant bowls of crisps and green olives.

Calle de Espronceda, 17, 28003, sylkarbar.com

Right and below: *The award-winning tortilla at Sylkar*

Cervecería El Doble

Named for the draft dobles the barmen swiftly serve, this small bar gets packed out quickly, as much for the aforementioned drinks as the fresh-looking seafood prepared at the bar. Styled as a traditional tavern with blue and white tiles (inside and out) and a marble bar, it's actually a baby, relatively speaking – some Madrid bars are over 100 years old – opening in 1987. However, it's probably the most famous bar on Calle de Ponzano, Chamberí's self-styled tapas street. The owner is something of a celebrity, appearing in what must be over 100 framed photographs that hang neatly on the walls, pictured surrounded by different combinations of smiling non-celebrity and celebrity guests who have frequented his bar over the decades. The opposite of a centuries-old dusty bar beloved of artists and stragglers, this one features bright blue strip lighting overhead and is freshly painted. Expect something small to eat with your first round of drinks, such as a silver tray of crisps or pickled mussels then try the rich red mojama, tongue-like salt-cured tuna served sliced and drizzled with olive oil then topped with a scattering of toasted almonds. There's also a larger brother bar on Alonso Cano.

Calle de Ponzano 58, 28003.

Bar Restaurante El Ponzano

The owner of this attractive bar and restaurant on the Chamberí street of the same name isn't the most welcoming, however the decor and food make it worth the struggle to get service with a smile. Sometimes you try, sometimes you don't. The secret is to not try too hard, just focus on the food, a combination of good quality raciones, pinchos and larger plates. The outside is painted in the red beloved of the classic Madrid tapas bar, while inside are brick walls, plants and well-spaced-out tables perfect for groups of tapas tours. Vegetarians and vegans

Hams hanging at the entrance to Bar Restaurant El Ponzano

The interior and patatas bravas in Bar Restaurant El Ponzano

may baulk at the large fridges on the way in, where huge hunks of meat hang, visible through the glass. Look at the menu instead, where you'll find an array of vegetable-based dishes from fried artichoke hearts to grilled asparagus, salmorejo and fried piparras (slim green chilli peppers). Please take note that when the Spanish refer to 'de verdura' 'meaning vegetables' they include Russian salad which is tuna-based... Beloved by carnivores and plant-based eaters alike are the made-to-order patatas bravas. Other bars have won awards, but these crispy, hot bites topped with a spicy tomato-based sauce and alioli are among the best in Madrid.

Calle Ponzano 12, 28010, restauranteponzano.com

El Fide

Packed out with local bar hoppers from around the area, this neighbourhood spot takes care with the preparation of its sought-after tapas dishes, with seafood a speciality. Anchovies come arranged in a lattice pattern on the

Above left, above right and below right:
Well-presented tapas at El Fide

plate – roll each fillet up and spear
with one of their toothpicks for easy
eating (then position a serviette
under your chin to catch the drips of
olive oil) – and thin white triangles
of smoked cheese are somehow
displayed with more precision here
than in many other bars. Order a draft
beer and a vermouth served with an
olive garnish, and you'll be rewarded
with a plate of crisps and a couple of
banderillas (small skewers of olives,
anchovies, gherkins and red peppers).
The well-stocked shelves behind the
bar display good looking arrangements

of canned delicacies such as tuna and anchovies in pretty cans and jars. You can sit in the main space on marble topped bar stools at high marble topped tables or head to the back for a more traditional sit down of larger plates at a table but perhaps with a little less atmosphere.

Calle de Ponzano 8, 28010.

La Vanduca

If you like to take your tapas in high-end surroundings, you'll love this bright restaurant, a five-minute walk from the Puerta de Alcalá (fun fact: a 1980s' song was dedicated to these landmark arches) in Salamanca. Run by four brothers from Malaga, the name is the unequal fusion of their two surnames, Van Dulken and Calleja, and nods to their Andalucian roots. It feels like a relaxed place where you could equally conduct business lunches or evening drinks, with a Mediterranean menu reflecting the Mediterranean decor by designer Sofía Calleja (clearly a relation). Well-placed touches of blue across the fabrics on banquette seating and on delicate ceramic plates, green on walls and a leafy patio to the front and rear create a holiday feel. Once you sit down, carafes of cold water and crisps come straight away, while you wait for dishes such as Padrón peppers – the small, bright green peppers fried

Opposite and above: *Aubergines and Padrón peppers at La Vanduca*

in extra virgin olive oil until they brown and blister, and mini chorizo sausages. If they are on the menu, which they are here, always order fried aubergines drizzled with honey after the most savoury or spicy item, as they are sweet and can take the place of dessert.

Calle Columela 2, 228001, https://lavanduca.es

Jurucha

We Brits are well known for queueing, the Spanish not so much. However, Madrileños are willing to line up for quite a while to secure a table at this slither of a long-established family-run bar, opposite the Mercado de la Paz, which is funnily enough where much of the ingredients come from. Well-dressed, well-coiffed older women snap

Locals queue for a table at Jurucha

their fingers at harassed waitresses once safely seated under the combined shade of square green umbrellas and centuries-old trees. If not, it's standing room only at the bar or eating at the dining space deep towards the rear, which means missing out on valuable people-watching opportunities, although the food is why you're here. Prices are higher here than in more spit and sawdust venues and some of the delicately presented portions of tapas are teeny, including dainty pintxos displayed in glass cases on the bar, such as small pieces of toasted bread piled high with sweet crab meat, creamy mayonnaise and slithers of briny pepinillo (pickled cucumber). Other morsels include half a hard-boiled egg topped with a prawn tail and a little dob of mayonnaise. Crowd-pleasing classics such as ensalada Rusa and a much-loved tortilla de patatas are also on the menu.

Calle Ayala, 19, 28001, jurucha.com

a.n.E.l Tapas & Lounge Bar

There's a romantic feel to this restaurant and bar, a five-minute walk from Parque del Buen Retiro, next to the French Embassy – perhaps that's why – from the long, illuminated bar, the centrepiece of the space, to

Right and overleaf: *Anel, a romantic bar for traditional tapas*

the splashes of modern art and the pretty terrace on the street. Eat your tapas sat on one of the high tables running the length of the bar, sipping an aromatic glass of vermouth served with a slice of orange – the waiters add a sense of occasion by pouring it at the table – and order a few media raciones (half portions). In summer, go for salmorejo, a creamy, cooling pinky-orange tomato soup topped with blobs of extra virgin oil, chopped egg and jamón, served in a tiny blue and white enamel dish. Follow up with montaditos (small sandwiches), which include tender solomillo de vaca vieja (sirloin steak) with melting brie. Also try the boquerones en vinagre – fresh anchovy fillets marinated in a mixture of vinegar and deep green extra virgin olive oil. Service is quick, even on a Friday lunchtime.

Calle de Villalar, 1, 28001, aneltapas.com

Casa Dani

One of the most famous places to eat at Mercado de la Paz, one of Madrid's longest-standing markets, is Casa Dani. This world-famous establishment, just off Calle de Serrano, has bragging rights to serving 'the best tortilla de patatas in Spain,' which is why locals will willingly queue for it. Not just the best in Madrid, note, but in the entire country. This no-frills family-owned restaurant churns out more than 200 tortillas a day. This variety is really gooey inside with a sweet onion meets fried potato mix oozing out onto the paper plate, yet it's well done on the outside. Order a pincho-size for a few Euros, a medio or an entire omelette; it's an any-time dish, designed for any appetite. Also try the albondigas, small lightly spiced meatballs made from pork in a rich gravy served with really

Below, opposite and overleaf: *Casa Dani's famous tortilla at Mercado de la Paz*

CASA DANI
EXTINTOR
COMIDA

RESTAURANTE
casa
DANI
CAFETERÍA

good crispy hand-cut chips. Aside from the famous tortilla, people come for the menu del día, posted daily on their social media. The portions are generous and come with plenty of bread. It fills up quickly at lunchtime so go early if you want to sit down at fuss-free tables covered with paper cloths – the good news is you can take it away, all boxed up.

Calle Ayala, 28, 28001, en.casadani.es

Bar Mirador El Estanque

You wouldn't necessarily come here for the tapas alone, but while you're taking in the unmissable green sprawl of Parque del Buen Retiro, why not sit at a table on the sandy floored terrace overlooking one of the best views in Madrid? Working well with the backdrop of the city's near permanent blue sky, locals and tourists row little light blue wooden boats on the green lake – one of the most visited parts of the green space – backed by the grandiose and almost ridiculously large stone monument to Alfonso XII; at his feet, steps lead down to the water. There are plenty of people-watching opportunities while you wait for your order from a menu rich in traditional favourites such as refreshing, salty and smooth gazpacho served in a glass, richly flavoured with olive oil and garlic. Typical tapas dishes such as patatas bravas and tortilla de patatas also make an appearance along with everyone's favourite blood-sugar-testing indulgence, chocolate con churros, deep fried sugar and cinnamon coated doughnut fingers dipped in a rich dipping chocolate.

Plaza de Venezuela, 5, Retiro, 28009.

Sip gazpacho at Bar Mirador overlooking the boating lake at Parque del Buen Retiro

Taberna & Media

This contemporary place to eat among the hotspots to the top end of the Parque del Buen Retiro is run by two generations of chefs, José Luis and Sergio Martínez. Some reviews say that the welcome is warm – in reality, this isn't always the case – but hearing the chef singing from the kitchen is always a good sign. Sit at the bar, tiled with mini-Mediterranean tiles and choose from the blackboard framed as if it were a picture, listing that day's recommendations. Fritter-style fusion patatas bravas defined by a creamy sauce are a firm favourite here, even winning an international award for the best in the world. The presentation is perfect on dishes whipped up with seasonal ingredients such as tajada de bacalao de la taberna, a juicy piece of cod encased in a golden battered coat served on an oval speckled white plate decorated with tiny purple flowers. To the rear, there's a brick-walled dining room with smart blue seats and homey plants on shelves overlooking a sweet little patio area. Fun fact: Robert De Niro cites this as his favourite place to eat in Madrid; Sergio Martinez worked at Nobu, a hospitality group the actor is a part owner of.

Calle de Lope de Rueda, 30, 28009, tabernaymedia.com

Below and opposite: *Taberna & Media is Robert De Niro's favourite Madrid tapas bar*

La Castela ●●●

Fun fact: Michelle Obama ate pinchos with her daughters here during a trip to Madrid. They would have dined among the older, well-off customers who swell the elegant interior of this Retiro bar and restaurant on a street that's home to some of the best in the area. Brass, mirrors, marble and gleaming white walls span the 60 years since it opened its doors in 1929 with a by-then much-needed makeover in 1989. Waiters flit from the bar to the kitchen, through the door out onto the tiny street-facing terrace and back, depositing plates and bringing you bill as they go. It's so popular that most of the tables are reserved, even at lunch, aside from a tiny marble shelf by the door and a few bar stools. Here, with a prime position in terms of seeing who comes in and out, be that waiters or clientele, you can rest your beer and generous portions of pinchos or raciones of staples such as a cheese board (tabla de quesos) with blobs of quince and raspberry jam and brittle little breadsticks. Freebies might include a saucer of smoked anchovies with a pair of Padrón peppers.

Calle del Doctor Castelo, 22, 28009, restaurantelacastela.com

Restaurante La Taberna De Buendi

The Calle del Doctor Castelo, a little to the north of Parque del Buen Retiro, near Ibiza Metro, doesn't have the bar-hopping reputation of streets such as Calle Ponzano. But it could. Among the multiple bars, this unassuming-looking spot bridges the gap between traditional and modern-style city venues. Decor-wise, it's light and bright, with a green palm-leaf mural running halfway up the walls and around the bar where chunky legs of ham hang from above and bottles of Spanish red wine decorate every surface – even above the door. The menu includes canapés and raciones, such as anchovies bathed in vinegar and olive oil, joined by juicy green olives and yellow green guindilla peppers, along with a plate of salty crisps. Far less expensive than its neighbours, this bar deserves more fame than it receives for the service and quality of food, but its regular clientele – mainly older retired men during weekdays – no doubt prefer it just as it is. The staff here are warmer than those in more celebrated bars and a tad speedier too, bringing your bill with a smile and, even better, a mini-ice cream or chocolate (like a treat for finishing your meal, which you will).

Calle del Doctor Castelo, 15, 28009, tabernabuendi.com

Above and below: *Staff at Restaurante La Taberna De Buendi dish traditional tapas with a smile*

Juan Antonio Doblado

Head Chef at Qú Restaurant by Mario Sandoval, JW Marriott Hotel Madrid.

From La Galantina restaurant in Salamanca to leading 100 chefs as part of the Sushita group, and Head Chef at the Sandoval brothers' two-Michelin-starred Coque Restaurant in Madrid, Juan Antonio Doblado has worked in the kitchens of some of the best restaurants in Spain. Now he's Head Chef at Qú by Mario Sandoval at the JW Marriott hotel in Plaza Canalejas, where all three Sandoval brothers work together, creating traditional dishes prepared with local products, as well as room service, 24 hours a day.

His five favourite tapas bars in Madrid are:

Casa Labra – founded back in 1860, this old tavern is an essential stop on any tapas tour. The freshly fried cod slices and croquettes are well worth the queue.

Docamar – don't miss this classic venue when you ir de tapear – the patatas bravas are the best in Madrid, fried to perfection and served with a secret spicy sauce.

Casa Lucio – famous for the huevos estrellados (chopped up fried eggs on hand cut chips) made with fresh

The Michelin-starred restaurant at JW Marriott Hotel Madrid

produce to order, these are always great. I love them with chistorra sausages on the side.

La Primera – although this is not 'strictly speaking' a bar, tapas in Madrid is inconceivable without tortilla de patatas and this restaurant's version is very special. Everything on the menu is made with wonderful fresh ingredients.

El Brillante – Open since 1961, this is the place to try Madrid's legendary calamari sandwich, but you must also try the Spanish omelette with tripe sauce on the side. The quality, service and cost are all excellent.

His favourite recipe is:
When summer comes, my kitchen at home is never without a jug of homemade salmorejo served with hard boiled eggs. This creamy cold tomato-based soup is one of many recipes that reflect how far a chef can elevate their cooking from the traditional recipe book. A little trick I use is to mix all the chopped ingredients, except the vinegar, the day before so that they macerate and take on as much flavour as possible. The next day, blend them all until well emulsified and pass through a fine strainer. Serve cold with the chopped boiled eggs on top. It's delicious and refreshing in the hot Spanish summer. This is how I make it at home:

1kg ripe vine tomatoes
180g white breadcrumbs
1 clove organic garlic
225g extra virgin olive oil
25ml sherry vinegar
100ml water
10g salt

MALASAÑA, CHUECA, SALESAS, PRINCESA & CONDE DUQUE

The unassuming Plaza del Dos de Mayo, at the heart of Malasaña, references the 2 May 1808 uprising, when Spanish soldiers and citizens fought Napoléon's invading troops. Two hundred years later, this happening district, close to central Sol, was the birthplace of the celebration of freedom known as La Movida Madrileña. The post-Franco movement revolutionised Spanish arts and culture and will forever be associated with film director Pedro Almodóvar. Once an old-school neighbourhood, home to the nanas and grandads born there, Malasaña has morphed into a place for pure, unadulterated fun, with a large student population, where street art isn't washed off walls and every week another new place to eat or drink opens. Sometimes such areas outprice the locals and lose their soul along the way, but if you take a good look around, you'll still find old-fashioned tapas bars and interesting places to shop such as the Mercado de Fuencarral, a youthful

shopping centre where young designers show off their latest creations, along with piercing and tattoo parlours. Next to Noviciado metro station there's a life-size bronze statue by Madrid-born sculptor Antonio Santín Benito of Julia, a young university student who attended the Universidad Central de la Calle de San Bernardo in the mid-nineteenth century disguised as a male, since only men were allowed access.

Flanked by Malasaña and Salesas, Chueca is the camp, beating heart of Madrid's LGTBIQA+ community and annual Pride festivals. The pink pound has largely been responsible for revitalising an area where gay couples and the older population walk their handbag dogs in tandem. Linger in the hulking Mercado San Antón, modernised in 2022, to try tapas from different regions of Spain alongside the well-rooted meat and fish stalls and a bar with a rooftop terrace. A cultural institution for those of us not fussed by museums, on the Chueca side of Gran

Colourful buildings in Malasaña, the old-school neighbourhood turned happening 'hood

Vía – though equally you could argue it's in Sol – Museo Chicote has been an institution since opening in 1931. This Art Deco legend, not a museum as the name implies, was where Frank Sinatra, Ava Gardner and Ernest Hemingway sank cocktails late into the night – is there a Spanish bar the boozey writer didn't drink at?

Today, you can still order his favourite cocktail, the Papa Doble. Overlooking the Plaza del Rey, here also is the Casa de las Siete Chimeneas, named for the chimneys that represent the seven deadly sins. Currently the Spanish Ministry of Culture, so you'll only see the outside, the sixteenth-century building is said to be haunted by the ghost of Elena, the daughter

of King Carlos V, who on hearing her secret lover had died at war, herself died of grief.

Set between upmarket Gran Vía, cooler Chueca and free-spirited Malasaña, Salesas is low on tourists which means it's high on the independent stores it's known for, such as specialist bookshops, haberdashers and organic food markets as well as authentic bars and restaurants, some Michelin-starred, some simple spots for a snack and a drink. The once bourgeois enclave is morphing into another of Madrid's happening districts. On the first Saturday of the month, local shops set up stalls on the streets creating a market called [The Festival] by SALESAS. Layered into the film-set like streets of Madrid's

Chueca, centre of the LGBTQ+ community in Madrid and with some of the city's most colourful cafes, restaurants and clubs

smallest barrio is a new crop of hotels, restaurants, and boutiques. Here also are cultural institutions such as the Museum of Romanticism, naturally housed in a pink eighteenth-century mansion. This period-furniture packed former palace allows a glimpse of how the Spanish bourgeoisie lived in the nineteenth century, and even the Magnolia Garden, landscaped in the French style, lends itself to romance along with a central fountain, a variety of shade-giving trees and wooden benches.

Conde Duque is a quieter area of cobblestoned streets, bars and independent stores. Set in a former brewery – the first Mahou beer brewery in Madrid – the Museo ABC features around 200,000 from 1890 until the present day; and free to enter. Here also, El Mercado de Los Mostenses is one of the best markets in the city, full of South American and Asian food stalls and produce.

Rubbing shoulders with Conde Duque, Princesa encompasses the remodelled and recently pedestrianised Plaza de España to one end of Madrid's main commercial artery, Gran Via. Here you'll find showy skyscrapers dwarfing tourist-free neighbourhood tapas bars just a street away. Recent renovations transformed the square into a more attractive, greener and accessible place to be with tree-shaded promenades and pedestrian paths to allow a connection between sites such as the Royal Gardens or the crowd-pleasing Templo de Debod (an Egyptian temple gifted brick-by-brick

The recently pedestrianised Plaza de España

to Madrid by the Egyptian government). During the summer free films are screened in the Plaza de España from 10pm, as the night cools down. To the western end, the 35-storey Torre de Madrid competes with the stepped red-brick facade of the Edificio España, built in the 1950s, which resembles US-style Art Deco towers.

Read on for a selection of places to eat for tapas lovers.

La Charca Taberna

On a side street in Princesa, just off the revamped Plaza de España, this restaurant is handy if you're off to see the Templo de Debod at sunset. It's a thing: you'll spot lines of people moving slowly as if in a trance towards the 2,000-year-old Egyptian structure in the Parque del Oeste. Despite the touristy location, La Charca is a humble taberna turned high-end dining spot, yet it retains the relaxed vibe you'd expect of a neighbourhood bar. Sit at the wooden bar or one of the high tables along the inside wall for tapas and a beer – whatever you drink, it will come with a nice free dish along the lines of vegetable-and-mayonnaise rich Russian salad (ensalada Rusa) served with

Potatoes with Cabrales cheese at La Charca Taberna

brittle bread sticks. The potatoes with creamy Cabrales cheese are delicious. There's a nice balance between the more traditional warm wood and brickwork with the added 1980s-style blue neon lighting a few Madrid bars seem to be favouring. The restaurant space towards the rear includes an attractive beamed and plant-filled internal courtyard for sampling larger Asturian dishes such as fabada, a rich, warming stew, studded with white beans and cachopo (two veal fillets layered with ham and cheese between then fried in breadcrumbs until crisp).

Calle de Juan Álvarez Mendizábal, 7, 28008, lacharcataberna.com

El Chiringuito Peruano, El Mercado de Los Mostenses

If you're craving – or want to try – authentic South American dishes in a quiet corner of Conde Duque for the first time, then this also-in-a-corner restaurant in the Mercado de Los Mostenses is for you. Served by the lovely Laura, a motherly figure who sits you down with toasted corn nuts and a little pot of chilli salsa before bringing homely meals such as papa rellenado, a golden crispy coated mass of potato encased beef mince. In many ways, it's effectively a giant, turbo charged croquette, made with mashed potato and served with a refreshing yet intensely flavoured salsa criolla, a red onion salad with chilies, lime juice and a few coriander leaves along with a dreamy custard-yellow sauce called huancaina. Made from aji amarillo, white cheese, oil, cream crackers and evaporated milk, yes really, eating the dish without this silky accompaniment would be like fish without tartar sauce. It's the ultimate comfort food served in a welcoming little restaurant.

Plaza de los Mostenses, 1, primera planta, local 9 y 10, 28015.

El Chiringuito Peruano at El Mercado de Los Mostenses

Taberna del Mozárabe ●●●

At night, this area, part residential, part commercial, in Conde Duque, morphs into a lively place to socialise. This isn't a bar you'll find on a 'Best Bars in Madrid' list, yet it should be among them. A five-minute-walk from the El Mercado de Los Mostenses, this old bar entices you, from the cheerful orange paint and tiled exterior with three doors opening onto the street, to the cheerful owner. Stained glass windows lend it a church-like charm as do free tapas served with a smile

Taberna del Mozárabe

by the owner, who must be among the most genial in Madrid. These include a wedge of tortilla on a hunk of bread and some green olives. The menu spans the juicy meatballs in tomato sauce, anchovies in oil and Russian salad visible on the bar along with that summer saviour, a tall glass of gazpacho, the perfect end to a hot day.

Calle de los Reyes, 6, 28015, tabefna-mozarabe.eatbu.com

Malpica

This charmer of a bar may be in Malasaña, just off the Plaza de Santa Maria Soledad Torres Acosta, a mouthful of a name for a residential square where children play and skateboarders skate, yet it's a far cry from Gran Vía, a couple of streets away. From the colourful menu featuring cacti, maracas and dancing couples to the wooden shelves set with old bottles, tile-topped tables, house plants and fresh flowers, the effect is to make you want to linger longer either in the smaller street-facing bar area or the set of rooms to the rear. Old park benches, exposed brick wall, bits of wrought iron propping up garden tables, groups of mirrors reflecting the light – this space has been well put together to create an eclectic homey feel welcoming customers from breakfasts

of churros and croissants to all-day tapas, lunch and dinner. Like the lively street it's on, the restaurant stays up late. The pincho of tortilla de patatas is one of the best to be had in the entire city, a generous portion of warm, slightly runny potato goodness served with a slice of good, fresh bread (in some bars, the side bread can be slightly stale). Part of the Bamboleo group, this bar is a good advert for the others dotted around the city centre.

Calle Corredera Baja de San Pablo, 4, 28004, malpicabar.com

Above and left: *The menu and tortilla at Malpica*

El Bar de San Antón

Hidden away on a side street in the Chueca district, among the gay-friendly nightlife, the Mercado de San Antón is a neighbourhood gastro-mecca. Designed to blend into the local architecture from the outside, inside it is shiny and modern with three floors of food and drink. El Bar de San Antón is the only bar among the good-looking deli-style counters on the first floor (nip up the escalators for an entire floor dedicated to tapas and easy-to-eat food). This is a sociable corner space for well-priced tapas dishes where you can choose to sit at the long communal table topped with red, yellow, green, black and white tiles or at the bar where glass cases reveal neat rows of tapas. The staff are friendly, allowing time to select from a menu that includes croquettes, which come as freshly fried foursome in a cute black basket, one truffle, one salt cod, one crab and one jamón.

Calle de Augusto Figueroa 24, 28004

El Bar de San Antón

Gota

It's hard to find – or is that easy to miss – this specialist wine bar in a peaceful part of the up-and-coming Salesas neighbourhood, on the border of Chueca. Almost a basement bar, you step down into it, ringing a doorbell to enter the well-thought-out place, both in design and concept, for wine-tasting, accompanied by tapas and a permanent DJ-played soundtrack. It's basically a low-ceilinged room with a large wooden bar with curved ends and two built-in decks, above the shelves sharing bottles of red wine and albums (readers under a certain age, these are vinyl). A few designer light-wood stools and chairs, walls covered with plaster and lime paint and black volcanic stone floors keep things minimal. To the rear is a cave-like vaulted space. The architect's pared-back dream is softened by candles lit at night. The menus are as simple as the decor – the wine menu divides into a few sparkling (burbujas), white and oranges in each category, and specialises in bottles from across Spain. Now then, orange wine may

Opposite, above and right: *Gota is a specialist wine bar with a small tapas menu*

need some explanation depending on your wine knowledge. Growing in popularity along with the natural wine movement, orange wine is made from white grapes that have the skin left on. It's not Tango-coloured but more amber. The small tapas-style menu is equally neat, with a few small plates with Italian touches, such as polenta fritters given a modern touch served fish-finger style with shavings of parmesan.

Calle de Prim, 5, 28004, gotawine.es

Golda

Yes, the cheery sunshine-yellow slightly seventies tiles around the counter of this Salesas cafe reflect the Madrid sun but also the disposition of the staff, who smile and make you feel welcome. It's fair to say that's not always the case in Madrid's many bars, restaurants and cafes. The rest of the space is light and whitewashed, with snug banquette seating and black Danish chairs, spanning an area by the street-facing window, another towards the rear with iron columns and a separate private event room with those sunny seventies tiles again. If you like R&B you're in luck as that's what's playing as you sip your specialty coffees or graze on a menu that mixes Argentinian and Israeli accents with Spanish elements in the large, perfectly round tortillas in the chiller cabinet along with bottles of lager and juices. There's a lot that's gluten free and vegan, from reviving smoothies packed with banana, tahini and date honey to falafel, shakshuka (although smoked salmon also features in bagels). Pets are allowed, men cuddle small dogs as they eat, and shelves contain earthenware tagines and design books.

Opposite, above and right: *At night Gota morphs from a cool café into a place for organic wines and tapas*

The name is a tribute to Golda Meir, the first female Prime Minister in Israel. Arrive at night and the cool cafe morphs into Golfa, a place for organic wines and tapas dishes at candlelit tables. The clue is on the back of the staff uniform – you guessed it, yellow t-shirts, printed with: 'Somos tarde y temprano' (we are early and late).

Calle de Orellana, 19, 28004, goldacafe.com

Rocafría

Madrid's neighbourhoods are forever changing; however, this bar-cafe-bakery is somewhere that remains the same. Perhaps this is why it attracts a continual stream of locals and the odd tourist for its good service, good food, but, above all, for its good-looking cakes. As you enter, staff greet you, which is just one more reason why it survives. Despite the prime location on Calle Barquillo in Salesas, overlooking the Palacio de Buenavista (now the army headquarters) and neighbouring the Only YOU Boutique Hotel, good value for money sandwiches, raciones and tapas include Russian salad, oreja and sepia a la plancha (fried pig's ear and squid) and torreznos. The look is part traditional, with a Mahou beer barrel and a long granite bar running the length of the space overhung with fake greenery, and part modern café with white formica tables by the window. Order a bocatin de jamón Ibérico and you'll get at least four layers of ham sandwiched between fresh baguette, moistened with olive oil. Glass cases house the real lure though: palmeras, sweet and flaky heart-shaped puff pastry cakes made in their own bakery, as well as roscón de reyes and churros. Sweet.

Calle del Barquillo, 20, 28004.

A multi-layered jamón Ibérico sandwich at Bocatin

El Tigre Sidra Bar

This Chueca stalwart isn't a place for people who follow a certain diet or worry about consuming double – or even treble – carbs. Oh no. Once through the door to the bar and you've ordered a beer or a cider from the speedy barman, you'll almost simultaneously receive an overloaded plate of hot and cold tapas. It's a bit like a food-based mission. Expect combinations of patatas bravas, mounds of yellow saffron rice (sometimes a bit soggy), slices of jamón serrano, chorizo and Galician Lacón ham on separate slices of baguette bread, Spanish omelette (also on sliced baguette), a couple of chicken wings, croquettes and whatever else they're offering on any particular day. Each plate varies (and gets bigger) with each round. The pub-like bar is boisterous, but it's also stuffy as there are no windows, only roaring air con units. The decor is on the dark side with varnished wooden tables, beams above and orange-painted or bare brick walls. Yet it's packed out on a July lunchtime, as no one is here for the interior design, despite the chi chi Chueca location. If you're on a tight budget, or you just like mounds of tapas, there's no better way to fill up for a few euros. If money's no object, and you just came in for a cool glass of beer or cider in a rowdy setting, you could try offering your plate to a hungry student.

Calle de Hortaleza, 23, 28004, bareltigre.es

A huge plate of free tapas at El Tigre Sidra Bar

Revoltosa

Fronting the photogenic Plaza del Rey in Chueca, this busy bar and restaurant is one of a pair of popular all-day dining spots, from brunches to burgers to tapas. Tapas are only available from 1pm (note: they will check the time, possibly letting you off if you arrive at 12.58) with twists on the traditional, such as Revoltosa Russian salad. This fusion version includes the usual potato and carrot, then takes a detour, moulded into a bagel shape with added parsnip, a homemade marinated caper 'mince' in the centre and jagged pieces of tuna sticking out of the top. This is less sickly than the standard recipe due to the earthiness of the beetroot and the homemade-style mayonnaise. The easy-on-the-eye decor is industrial-vintage – grey-painted iron pillars hold up the ceiling where old-fashioned weighing scales are suspended, upcycled into planters for faux ferns, art deco lamps and bentwood chairs. Pigeons scuttle about picking up crumbs off the mosaic-tiled floors – they enter via the folding doors that push right back for an appealing indoor/outdoor effect. Best reserve a table on the terrace overlooking the square, with a hint of greenery and a cooling fountain, which livens up during Pride each year and the film shoots that mean it gets cordoned off from time to time.

Plaza del Rey 4, 28004, revoltosamadrid.com

An earthy take on Russian salad at Revoltosa

Fermentera

True to its name, this small-ish bar in the heart of Chueca feels like you could arrive in your beachwear, towel in hand, sand sticking to your feet. Aiming to bring the flavours of the Balearic Islands to central – landlocked – Madrid, the decor is fittingly relaxing with white painted brickwork and Scandi-ish

FIGUEROA
Fermentera
BAR BALEAR
Fermentera
BAR BALEAR
Fermentera
BAR BALEAR
illy
L10

lightwood tables and chairs. The marble bar is the main attraction, set with delicious dishes of gildas (little, green-themed skewers of olives, anchovies and guindilla peppers), silver-brown anchovies resting in olive oil, and thick chunks of crispy crackling. From the islands, there are also piles of pastry empanadas and thin and crispy cocas, flatbreads topped with skinny-cut slices of courgette and tomato. In the back corner, there's a mini delicatessen space with wooden shelves stocked with bottles of wine, garlands of garlic pinned to the wall, and a chiller cabinet with large round cheeses and cured meats for customers to sample seated at the high tables. For parties or meetings in less corporate surroundings, the basement space can be booked for events.

Calle Augusto Figueroa 22, 28002, barfermentera.com

Perretxico Chueca

Basque chefs are known for their genius in the kitchen; there are proportionally more Michelin-starred restaurants in the Basque Country than anywhere in the world. Not only that, but the pintxo is also a firm pillar of Basque dining. Pintxos tend to feature ingredients layered on top of a piece of bread speared with a cocktail stick. Combining both Basque traditions of fancy food and small bites in one, chef Josean Merino has long been the

Basque pintxos at Perretxico Chueca

king of the pintxos, from his original Basque restaurant to the four Madrid restaurants, with plans to roll out more branches around the country. The decor is minimal, different in each branch; the Chueca version is a light-filled space set with light wooden tables and chairs, plus arrangements of cowbells on walls, which relates to the zanpanzar, a character from Basque folklore and the spirit of carnival. Coining the phrase pintxocultores, Merino even offers a pintxo tasting menu in his restaurants. It feels like fast food with heritage. Glass counters display immaculately created small dishes, the presentation arty and more Michelin-starred than MacDonald's. A gilda is served like a figure of a person, the head an olive, the peppers arms, the Cantabrian anchovy wrapped around the body; a soft, easy to spoon-in egg and prawn combination mixed with strained yoghurt from Donosti is served in a ceramic eggshell (both feature on the tasting menu).

Calle Augusto Figueroa 32, 28004, perretxico.es

Bodegas El Maño

Even on a Monday night at 9.30pm there might only be one or two tables left as this traditional bar close to the Plaza de España packs out; so, reserve a table if you don't want to wait for long. The winning combination of a relaxed atmosphere with good-looking interiors – marble-topped tables and art deco touches offset by faded, yellowed paintwork – and on-the-money tapas and wines by the glass makes it a hit with locals in the know and tourists who are lucky enough to chance up on it. Oh, and the staff are really efficient too. Originally part of a family-run group of vineyards, today only this central spot in Conde Duque remains. Many restaurants and bars are known for one or two specialties, whereas pretty much every dish here is worth trying. Order patatas bravas – cubes of fried potatoes coated in a smoky paprika-rich tomato sauce and a glass of Spanish wine (available by the glass or bottle and chalked up on blackboards). In the summer, the three sets of French windows open onto the street so you can soak up the street life as you work your way through the menu including the tortilla de patatas, which shows how you can create a masterpiece with just a few eggs and potatoes.

Calle de la Palma, 64, 28015, bodegaselmano.com

Bodega La Ardosa

Attempting to eat and drink in this teeny, red-painted bar awash with centuries-old memories, faded framed photos hanging on walls and dusty wine bottles, is a little like a game of Twister. Diners of all ages cram around wooden barrels-turned-tables in this old-school tapas bar where you ignore the lack of space for the

charm of smashed artichokes seeped in extra virgin olive oil then crisped on a hot plate and runny *tortilla de patatas* made to the owner's mother's recipe so special it's won awards (you can find the recipe on their website and have a go.) You'll

find yourself constantly moving around to accommodate newcomers sharing your space or staff bringing tapas dishes. Peek behind the bar and another slightly less crowded back room is reachable only by ducking under the wooden bar as you dodge staff juggling plates of hot food and/or pouring glasses of draft Pilsner or vermouth. It opened in 1892 and much of the decor is original, from the tiled walls

Bodega La Ardosa is old-school tapas bar in the heart of Madrid

to the vintage beer and spirit bottles on shelves.

Calle de Colón, 13, 28004, laardosa.es

Pez Tortilla

This modern take on a neighbourhood tapas bar is part of a chain of five, all in Madrid, created by four friends whose mission statement is: 'There are two types of people in life. Those who like slightly curdled potato omelettes and those who have no fucking idea about

Above and opposite: *Pez Tortilla is a modern take on a neighbourhood tapas bar*

life.' Naturally, it feels independent. The original venue still looks fresh with a simple monochrome scheme of smart white metro tiles and a black marble bar, but the millennial clientele don't put up with being elbow-to-elbow for the interiors. It's all about what's chalked up on the blackboards, washed down with craft beer. Order to the right of the bar, then sit on a high stool or stand at the handful of small white bistro tables. It doesn't matter, as the garlicky tortilla is the star of the show. It's runny inside, which isn't to everyone's taste, filled with clever combinations of truffle, jamón, brie and goat's cheese. Don't forget about the crunch-coated croquettes filled with carrillada (beef cheek stew) and creamy bechamel, with the outsides nicely browned. The wine list mirrors the food menu, with a few choice labels including Monopole (a white Rioja), and there's a wider selection of around 30 local and imported craft beers.

Calle Pez, 36 28004, peztortilla.com

Raul Garcia Molina

Executive Chef at Hilton Madrid Airport.

Born in Madrid, Raul studied culinary arts at the prestigious Hospitality School, before becoming chef for the French ambassador in Madrid. He then moved on to Basque cuisine kitchens such as Illunbe in La Moraleja and Lur Maitea in Madrid. He has also worked in England at Spanish restaurant Cambio de Tercio, and participated in International Paella Competitions in Sueca, Valencia.

Growing up as the son of a chef, Raul was surrounded by cookbooks, sparking a deep curiosity that led him to absorb every recipe he could find. His childhood was a culinary adventure, with every book opening a new world of flavours and techniques.

His five favourite tapas bars in Madrid are:

Taberna La Dolores – start your Madrid tapas tour at this classic spot, famous for the best anchovies and boquerones paired with an exceptionally poured beer.

Casa Revuelta – the go-to place for the finest fried cod, with a delicate and crispy batter.

El Quinto Vino – located just outside of the city centre, known for its impressive croquettes and delicious stews like rabo de toro (oxtail) and callos. It also features an excellent wine menu and a distinctly Madrilenian atmosphere.

La Casa del Abuelo – this iconic establishment's philosophy starts with its famous prawns, whether grilled or al ajillo, perfectly complemented by a chilled white wine.

Casa Toni – another emblematic Madrid bar, celebrated for its monumental grilled pig's ear with garlic and parsley, served with a delicious brava sauce.

His favourite recipe is:

Cod slice with pork terrine and prawns on brioche

This is a dish that I regularly make at home. I love it because it layers so

Raúl García Molina

many different flavours and techniques. This sandwich is a unique mix of sweet and salty flavours. It is easy to serve in slices and perfect in our long hot Spanish summers as a tapa.

Cook the pork cheek with vegetables and aromatics (carrot, onion, leek, celery, whole peppercorns, cloves). Once tender, drain it and make a terrine with the meat, leaving it to chill in a mould in the fridge overnight. Cut two 10 x 3 cm, 1 cm thick rectangles from brioche bread. Grill them and set them aside. The next day, cut a slice of the terrine the same size as the brioche bread and grill it on both sides.

Marinate the prawns with a mixture of garlic, pepper, choricero pepper paste and parsley, letting them marinate overnight. Grill them ready for assembly.

With the cod, make a packet with filo dough the same size as the brioche bread and the pork snout terrine.

Finally, begin layering the sandwich: brioche bread, pork snout terrine, fried cod in filo pastry and another piece of brioche bread. Place the grilled prawns on top once the sandwich is closed. Garnish with parsley and enjoy!

Cod

10g cod loin
A whole garlic bulb
100gm filo pastry
75g choricero pepper paste
2g ground cumin parsley, dried chilli, sweet paprika

Terrine

500g pork cheek
300g onions
200g carrots
100g celery salt, peppercorns, cloves
200g tiger prawns
A few slices of brioche bread

LOS AUSTRIAS, SOL-GRAN VÍA & BARRIO DE LAS LETRAS

The good-looking clutch of palaces, squares and ornamental gardens of Los Austrias, so-called because many of them were built during the reign of the Austrian Habsburgs, is a visual history lesson. This is an area of scaled-up, impressive architecture where tourists stop snapping selfies to

Gran Vía, a grand boulevard lined with towering belle-époque facades, cuts through much of central Madrid

watch crowd-pleasing break dancers outside the sizeable Royal Palace with around 3,000 rooms built to dwarf its European counterparts. What isn't on the tourist trail despite being right next to the palace (many locals don't even know about them) are the remains of the Muslim Walls of Madrid. The Parque del Emir Mohamed I, named after the Moorish king who built the walls dating back to the ninth century, is only open at weekends, but their crumbly white bricks are visible through the gates.

Local landmarks also include the Sabatini Gardens, which are part of the Palace, with fittingly fine symmetrical terraces, sculptures, cooling fountains, mazes and a pond. When Madrid becomes unbearably hot for most, you can sit for a while, fanning yourself in the shade of a tree and dreaming of autumn.

If the snug network of medieval streets that make up central Madrid feels too much, the nearby Plaza Mayor is an almost ridiculously large

The Habsburg-designed Plaza de Mayor is a grand square with a storied history and close to dozens of tapas bars

cobblestoned square (although strictly speaking it is a rectangle), where over the centuries a morally mixed bag of slave markets, bullfights, Spanish Inquisition trials and multiple royal ceremonies have filled the space over the years; and today, the purpose has switched to more mindful events such as yoga workshops and Christmas markets. It's a good-looking place of deep orange painted apartments dressed in wrought iron balconies. During the nineteenth century, a market stall from Alicante selling turrón grew so popular that the owners were able to open Casa Mira's rosemary honey, sugar, egg and almond-scented doors on the square by 1855. A battered, blackened 150-year-old manual machine is still used to toast the almonds over a gas flame; the original nineteenth century green metal columns still prop the shop up. What we call nougat in English, although Spanish turrón is crunchier and more brittle, is revered in Spain as the ultimate Christmas gift (my Spanish family used to send a few packets of it over every year), which means this is one shop that will never go out of business.

The area between Puerta del Sol and Gran Vía is the beating heart of Madrid in many ways. Puerta del Sol –

Ancient arches leading onto side streets surrounding Plaza Mayor, a symbol of the city

or simply Sol to locals – is also the symbolic centre of Spain. A plaque in front of the clock tower reads 'Kilometre Zero,' marking the point where all distances are measured from. The Oso y el Madroño statue of a Bear nuzzling a strawberry tree – the stuff of fridge magnets and tea towels – is a handy meeting point. Step away from such approved official tourist landmarks, and you can find arguably more interesting sights, such as pockmarks from bullets fired during the Civil War in the white stone and brick Regional Government of Madrid building. Shift sideways, between Puerta del Sol and Gran Vía, to 30 Calle de la Montera. Above a sex shop here is the looping graffiti sprayed by Muelle, a pioneer in the street art movement in Madrid during the 1980s-born post-Franco *Movida Madrileña*. Dodge the shoppers along Gran Vía, on the corner of Calle Alcalá and look up at the Edifício Metrópolis, a photogenic unofficial symbol of the city you'll see in any article about Madrid. You can understand why it's so photographed, all French-style curves, from the cylindrical facade to the slate dome, sculptures and garlands. A gold-tipped figure – the Winged Victory – crowns the building.

The surrounding streets are where you'll find authentic tapas bars that are long-time favourites with locals, particularly in the triangular district formed between Puerta del Sol, Plaza

The statue of King Philip III on horseback at the heart of Plaza Mayor

Puerta del Sol is the symbolic centre of Spain and a famous meeting point

Mayor and Plaza de Santa Ana. You could spend days nipping in and out of the bars and restaurants in the area. While you do, stop to nose in the window of Santos Seseña on Calle de la Cruz. Even if your taste isn't for dramatic swishy capes – if you're neither a bullfighter nor an opera singer, why would it be? – these colourful handmade garments are historical. Picasso was buried wrapped in one while Hillary Clinton had one tailor made.

Then there's the Barrio de las Letras (Literary Quarter), a cuter, smaller unofficial barrio with a strong literary connection, once home to the revered seventeenth-century Spanish writers such as Lope de Vega and Cervantes. The streets are paved with snippets of quotes on golden brass letters forged onto the pavement on Calle Huertas, with plazas and streets are dedicated to them. This is the main artery of the neighbourhood, lined with some of the oldest bars in Madrid and also some of the newest. Here, one of the best-looking spots in the city – the glamorous Plaza de Santa Ana – is steeped in arts and culture of all types. At one end there's the Teatro Español, where a statue of murdered twentieth-century poet and playwright Federico García Lorca holds a bird in his hands, while at the other the ME Madrid Reina Victoria, housed in a modernist nineteenth-century building, presides over the square as if carved in thick white icing. Tapas

The leafy Plaza de Santa Ana is home to a theatre and multiple tapas bars

bars, from old wood panelled ones to modern art-filled spaces line the square, most with large terraces that spray cold water mist in summer. On the first Saturday of each month, the Mercado de las Ranas (Frog Market) is a flea-style market like Campden, In North London named after the frogs in the ponds of the orchards of the old Convent of San Jerónimo.

Read on for a selection of places to eat for tapas lovers.

Los Galayos

Everyone knows the Plaza Mayor is not where you go to eat, with inflated prices and frozen paellas served up in suspiciously short amounts of time - anyone eating here will come away with a dim view of Spanish food. However, Los Galayos, a tardis-like, family-run restaurant on the edge of the famous square, is well worth a visit. There's a lot of it to contend with, three floors divided into a couple of bars – one hand-carved in the seventeenth-century – and plenty of dining spaces combining rich red walls, vaulted ceilings, rustic beams and a tiled outside terrace with heaters for colder climes. Suckling pig is the thing to eat here, and it makes it onto the tapas menu, which is full of pinchos and raciones, in the form of roasted and fried (note both forms of cooking) ears. The tortilla de patatas

is of the runny variety and perhaps lacks seasoning but it's still a good dish. Different from the British black pudding, the morcilla here comes with a side of pisto (ratatouille), served in thick rounds, like small patties packed with puffed up rice. Order tiny

paelleras of patatas revolconas con sus choricitos y torreznillos, mashed potatoes turned orange as if made with sweet potato from the paprika and chorizo. Wines such as white Albariño or red Rioja go with whatever you choose. Waiters are machine-like in their undivided attention and stamina, running up and down the stairs, so stand to one side if you see one with a pot of something hot.

Calle de Botoneras, 5, 28012, losgalayos.net

Los Galayos, a family-run restaurant on the edge of Plaza Mayor

Restaurante Gloria Bendita

There's a fun and global feel to this industrial-meets-eclectically kitted-out bar not far from Mercado de San Miguel in Los Austrias. We're talking sturdy iron pillars, vintage-style amber Edison light bulbs, open-brick walls and a slightly random 1970s-era television. From the bossa nova tunes humming in the speakers to the map of the world on the wall, trailing foliage and potted palms and holiday snaps on a pin board, even if you live in Madrid, once in the door, you'll feel you're on holiday. A sign with the message: 'If the ice in your drink is melting, you're not drinking fast enough' encourages this vibe. Snack on a small pot of green olives while you sip a cold beer and choose your tapas. It's all flavoursome and well presented, from chargrilled meaty broad beans from Granada with strips of salty ham, fried eggs and a scattering of black pepper on top to a plate of thin-cut Bellota cured ham. Other traditional dishes on the QR-code available menu include octopus, patatas bravas and croquettes. The outside seating area has attractive rattan chairs among the the plants and parasols on the patio.

Calle de Santiago, 3, 28013, gloriabenditarestaurante.com

Holiday vibes and tapas at Gloria Bendita

Taberneros

The red-painted frontage – there's a matching bar inside – will charm you to stop at this well-established bar in the Literary Quarter. It says 'tradition', as much as the brick walls and wooden floor-lined interiors, and rest assured staple Spanish tapas dishes feature on the menu, as does a traditional cocido stew every Thursday. However, there's fusion here too with Russian salad ramped up with wasabi mayonnaise and smoked salmon tartar. Multiple bottles of wines from around Spain

Taberneros is a well-established bar in the Literary Quarter

line the walls and fill racks; the cellar has 300 with sommeliers on hand to advise. If your eyesight is good, you can browse as you sample crispy croquetas de pringá, the usual cylindrical shape switched for small balls filled with a soft mixture of Iberian ham and peas. Order a couple of cañas and you'll receive a few tiny dishes to snack on, such as crisps, olives and gerkins.

Calle de Santiago, 9, 28013.

Casa Revuelta

Just off the Plaza Mayor, Casa Revuelta is a blink-and-you-miss-it bar that feels like it's been around forever. A relative newcomer compared to the 100-year-old bars – owner Santiago Revuelta opened its doors in 1966. Madrid excels in places like this, which fly in the face of those that charm with quaintly painted exteriors or atmospheric olive tree-clad patios and yet get packed out every night for a few simple dishes. The dishes in question are golden fried salt cod made from a secret recipe passed from generation to generation, and crunchy torreznos (pork crackling). While you stand elbow-to-elbow at the bar, a bit like being a shopper in the January sales, check out the original Moorish-style mustard tiles, dark wooden ceiling and silver bar, or just nose at what everyone else is having. Staff, who are the same age as the retired clientele who you're fighting

Above and right: *Free tapas of bread and cheese and gildas at Casa Revuelta*

for space with, calmly pour thimbles – stemless glasses known as chatos – of full-bodied Spanish red such as Valdepeñas. Free tapas might be hunks of bread and cheese or gildas, green peppers, olives and anchovy skewers. There's a sister restaurant nearby so it's easy if you want to stay loyal while creating a mini tapas bar crawl.

Calle de Latoneros, 3, 28005, casarevuelta.com

Revuelta

This slightly more polished version of the original big brother bar Casa Revuelta, opened in 2021 as a more spacious, more youthful counterpart. Revuelta feels more like a wine bar, with shiny white metro tiles and shelves of Spanish wines joining the hanging hams and tempting jugs of Sangria. In contrast to Casa Revuelta, as well as the decor, the staff here are younger and mainly women. There's more space to sit – choose from along the bar, at high or low tables or outside on the terrace. Parents bring their kids; friends meet for a night out and tourists swarm past *en route* to the Plaza Mayor. Free tapas include patatas alioli, lightly fried potatoes covered in a warm, garlicky mayonnaise, but the star of the show is still the battered boneless cod (bacalao revuelto).

10 Calle Cuchilleros, 28005, casarevuelta.com

Mesón del Champiñón

A couple of streets away from the Plaza Mayor, the 'house of the mushroom' name implies this is a temple to all things fungi related. In fact, it's not, but it doesn't matter as the owners do a few things – strictly speaking only two things with mushrooms – really well. Grilled on a hot plate, the mushrooms come stuffed with cubes of chorizo, chopped garlic and parsley, oil, lemon and salt, or vegetarian, e.g. minus the chorizo. Each mushroom is served spread with a pair of toothpicks so you can kind of engineer it into your mouth (grab a serviette to hold under your chin as it gets messy, the juices dripping downwards). The result is a smokey, juicy snack that is surprisingly morish, however Padrón peppers and croquettes are also on the menu. The slim bar and restaurant are housed in a thick castle-like structure, entered via

Grilled and stuffed mushrooms at Mesón del Champiñón

a hole in the wall for a door. There's a dad joke opportunity to say there's not mushroom in there. Maybe not. Stand at the bar under a giant wooden beam and watch the chef grill or sit in the small cave-like dining space to the rear. Look up and note the mushroom-like shapes on the ceiling, as if the main attraction has been thrown upwards.

Cava de San Miguel, 17, 28005, https://mesondelchampinon.com/en/

La Casa del Bacalao

If you enter the Mercado de San Miguel from the direction of the Plaza Mayor, this is one of the first stalls you'll see. La Casa del Bacalao, meaning the House of Cod, unsurprisingly specialises in all things cod, which you can sample on tapas starting at an appealingly low price. The presentation is immaculate: glass cases reveal rows of bread slices topped with sardines, anchovies, Galician octopus, smoked salmon and cod foie gras lying on a strip of red pepper or cheese. Everything is served on blue and white paper plates and staff sport smart blue and white t-shirts. Behind them are rows of shelves of prettily packaged tins of smoked, salt-cured and tinned herring, salmon and anchovies from Denmark, Norway and Northern Spain lined up above the blue and white tiles. The stall is part of a chain, with shops

La Casa del Bacalao at the Mercado de San Miguel

around Madrid and another at the Mercado San Antón in Chueca. Stand wherever you find a space and decide whether you want to order another – you will – or be more Spanish and move on to one of the many stalls here; alternatively take it away if you prefer a bit more space when you eat.

Mercado de San Miguel, lacasadelbacalao.es

Taberna Real

Well placed between Sol and the Palacio Royal among the regality of Las Austrias, this corner spot on the Plaza de Isabel II (named for the queen whose turbulent life included marrying her gay cousin, six of her 11 children dying and eventual exile to France) was once where the royal staff lived. In 1969, the Pardellas Rivera brothers opened a restaurant, and generations continue to cook, pour drinks and serve. Walls are painted pea green, with decor from a set of hanging violins and a harp from the Teatro Royal, copious amounts of tiles on walls, floors

Tapas at Taberna Real

and, behind the curved marble bar, even a portrait of mama and papa Pardellas Rivera. An oversized crystal chandelier sparkles above the bar, a replica of one that hangs in the nearby palace today, where vats of green and black olives share the space with classic hams. This is a place people come for the fruity vermouth on tap and generous amounts of well-known tapas dishes such as wafer-thin slices of jamón Ibérico topped with toasted almonds. There's another slightly more formal dining space upstairs.

Plaza de Isabel II, 8, 28013, tabernareal.com

Tapaspaña

Despite having the brightly lit look and feel of a fast-food chain or a Benidorm tourist trap, which mainly comes from the dozens of laminated photographs of dishes at the entrance, this busy Gran Vía bar just off the Plaza de

Tapaspaña is a busy bar just off the Plaza de España

España deserves a closer inspection. Once inside, attentive waiters are quick to seat you, take your order and serve good-looking plates of well-presented tapas and raciones, from seafood to charcuterie and, of course, tortilla de patatas. To be fair, it does also nod to tradition, with a deli-style station with rows of ham legs strung above cured sausages hanging in loops and bottles of Spanish red while the curved, white-tiled bar, whitewashed brick walls and blue metal chairs veer more towards a modern industrial look. Prettily patterned plates lined with deep-fried battered anchovies served with lettuce and a jagged-cut lemon half to squeeze over them and offset the fried element are perfect for sharing, but you'll want to keep your glass of chilled sangria to yourself.

Calle Gran Vía, 73, 28013.

La Casa del Abuelo

The original outpost of this family-run collection of bars and restaurants has been going strong since 1906. The Calle de la Victoria branch is the original but there are seven in total so far including a vineyard in Zamora province in the Castilla y León region of Spain and a sister restaurant opposite, so close the outside dining spaces almost merge. Mainly older male staff charm with speedy service and humour as they fetch chairs to accommodate a larger group

Left, above and overleaf: *The family-run La Casa del Abuelo*

while avoiding burning diners as they ferry earthenware dishes of their famous gambas al ajillo – sizzling prawns in garlic-infused olive oil from the kitchen to the large terrace (sometimes from bar to bar). Be sure to mop up the flavoured oil before you let them whisk the dish away. This dish has more significance than just a popular tapa. Originally a sandwich shop, the owners invented during the gruelling Civil War years when Franco's ring around the city meant getting food supplies into the capital became increasingly difficult and there was no bread.

After the prawns, move onto large portions of perfect wafer-thin squares

Casa Toni ●●●

On a skinny side street, a couple of blocks from Puerta del Sol, this old-school spot smells of fresh lemon and frying food as you enter. The small space fills up with regulars every single day, a combination spanning well-off locals and students. Downstairs, pink walls with blue and white tiles below are hung with decades of wonkily hung framed matador-related photos and faded newspaper cuttings. There's a couple of small tables to sit at, stand at or else you can prop up at the bar; upstairs there's more space to sit and eat but a little less atmosphere. It stays loyal to its clientele from all walks of life who cram in for affordable Spanish staples such as the nose-to-tail crackling-style pigs' ears (oreja a la plancha), riñones (kidneys) and lamb sweetbreads (mollejas). If you're squeamish, order the prettier prawns (gambas al ajillo) swimming in hot olive oil infused with chilli flakes, lemon juice and garlic sprinkled with a chopped parsley garnish. Welcoming staff swiftly serve glasses of richly-coloured fruity vermouth and cold draft beers with free tapas including slices of crusty white bread joined by a few chunks of bright pink lacón (ham from Galicia or Asturias).

Calle de la Cruz, 14, 28012.

of jamón (cured ham) and a salad of large, sliced sun-ripened tomatoes topped with chopped garlic, parsley and a good glug of olive oil. Tables fill up quickly on Saturdays, but you won't wait that long to be squeezed in somehow, somewhere. Inside, it's standing room only at tiny marble shelves and high tables, and those prawns even feature as a design in tiles on the walls. Note the prettily painted names of dishes on the windows which regularly feature on Instagram.

Calle de la Victoria, 12, 28012, lacasadelabuelo.es

Casa Toni fills up with regulars every day

Tapas & Más

Despite the modern wine bar feel, this restaurant is housed in an ancient building with charm and character coming from the open brick walls and arched vaulted areas in the basement. There's a small terrace on the streets running along both sides. Tapas dishes come served in teeny paella pans – go for the huevos rotos con jamón – a blissful medley of a fried egg on top of hot hand-cut chips draped with ham, a dish said to go back to 1605 when Don Quixote of La Mancha in Miguel de

Tiny dishes at Tapas y Mas

Cervantes' groundbreaking novel tucks into a daily plate. Who can blame him? You can't go wrong with ham, egg and chips, which is effectively what this dish is, just deconstructed, Spanish-style. Huevos rotos translates literally as broken eggs and rightly so in this case as the Spanish style is to break up the fried egg, so the soft yoke coats the potatoes underneath. The pair of croquetas caseras is just the right amount of what can be a sickly dish – crisp on the outside filled with a salty, cheesy, jamón bechamel and perfect with a glass of Rioja from the bar.

Calle de Espoz y Mina, 18, 28012, https://tapasymas.net

Emma Cocina

Easy to find, just behind the wrought-iron gourmet-stall-lined Mercado de San Miguel, this is an unassuming bar for a relaxed glass of wine in modern surroundings – despite the misleading old wine barrel outside. Sit at Scandi-style wooden tables flanked by the old industrial black columns among in-the-know locals and order a glass of Rueda (a dry white wine) or a Ribera vino tinto from the daily-changing blackboard. You'll be rewarded with a free serving of a tapa, such as creamy Russian salad on thinly sliced crusty white bread. The menu is simple, with a handful of dishes, which is always a good sign, and includes classic homestyle dishes with low prices piled high on plates, such as tenderly stewed beef cheek with creamy mashed potato. Also try the all-Spanish cheeses such as Valdeón, a blue cheese made from cow's and goat's milk in the Picos de Europa mountains or Manchego dressed with rich olive oil and served with bite-sized breadsticks. If you like the wines that much, you can buy a bottle to go. It's rare to see a tourist here despite the location so close to their usual Madrid hangout, around the heaving Plaza Mayor.

Plaza de San Miguel, 4, 28005.

Hearty dishes and Spanish wine at Emma Cocina

La Carmela

Just off Puerta del Sol, in the beating heart of touristy Madrid, this corner spot has a lot to offer. Part of the Hotel Quatro Puerta del Sol, 100m away, the red-painted restaurant has a generous terrace, which wraps around the side street. It's no beauty, but a nice enough place to sit if you're in the sun. When you enter, however, it's another thing altogether, an attractive bistro-style space with potted palms, Mediterranean tiles on the floor and ancient brickwork. Waiters dash in and out bringing bargain croquettes and generous portions of patatas bravas, not in a red sauce but smothered with a pleasingly picante spicy brown version mixed with creamy alioli, that would feed two or three people. Like many central Madrid bars, it also specialises in callos and cocido madrileño. The terrace fills up quickly even on a weekday lunch. Come at night to watch live flamenco shows while you eat in the old, vaulted brick coal cellars below.

Calle Victoria, 4, 28012, tabernalacarmela.com

El Rincón Abulense

The average tourist wouldn't think to stop off at this missable barrio bar on a scruffy street just off Gran Vía. They'd only go if they'd been told to. Now you know you can join the locals standing at the bar or be seated in the middle restaurant area or the back space. The latter feels a bit like a badly decorated front room with a television that's always on, but with the sound down, of course, sharing a wall with multiple volumes of books and encyclopaedias. This space gets busy at lunchtime with locals filling up on the homestyle three-course menu al día, brimming with hearty dishes such as smokey lentil stew, barbecued tender ribs and soft veal scallops. It's famed for the generous tapas that come with every round of drinks. Order a beer and a basket of bread and breadsticks appears simultaneously along with a croquette (not always warm and not always the best to be honest but if you like a little free food with your drink, you'll not complain). Better tapas are juicy meatballs and chorizo they also serve swiftly and generously.

Calle del Caballero de Gracia, 18, 28013.

En Busca de Tiempo

You can take your pick of the many bars shoulder to shoulder along the side streets surrounding Puerta del Sol, such as Calle de Cádiz and Calle Barcelona, which make up Madrid's old town. Effectively, it creates a ready-made tapas trawl. If you're in the mood to sit and watch the world go by, which may mean just a few people across the street eating and drinking and the odd delivery man lugging bottles of water or wine up or down the street, then this is a good place to sit out on the terrace. Order a beer and the nice waiters bring you briny olives and mini pickles while you 'um' and 'ah' over the pretty extensive menu. If you venture inside to the bar and restaurant space, you'll find traditional hams hanging and on stands ready for carving, old wooden beams, warm shades of orange and contemporary tiles. Like your wine? Bottles are displayed in every available space, encased in glass, on shelves and behind the smart bar. Upstairs there's another slightly more rustic dining space with an old brick chimney in one corner. And note the bifold doors are

pulled wide back in warmer weather so rest assured you don't miss out on people-watching opportunities.

Calle Barcelona, 4, 28012, enbuscadeltiempo.es

La Descubierta

Locals and tourists rock up at midday to this red-painted bar wedged in among all the others on Calle Barcelona, which runs all the way from Puerta del Sol to Calle de las Huertas, the hub of the Barrio de las Letras. Sit in the sun on the plastic chairs on the cobblestoned terrace or head inside

Below and overleaf: *La Descubierta draws locals and tourists*

for the warm interior combination of sunshine-yellow walls and open brickwork. This is good value tapas – a generous plate of thick-cut jamón de recebo, a cheaper version of bellota, cured for less time but with a rich flavour, aboard a huge slice of bread topped with tomatoes grated, mixed with olive oil and salt. A bottle of rich green extra virgin olive oil is placed on the table so you can drizzle it on top for extra flavour. Beware of al fresco smokers to your right – the smell can waft downwind.

Calle Barcelona, 12, 28012.

Castizo Alcalá-Canalejas

Opposite Seville Metro, this attractive space is part of a chain of Madrid restaurants. Sit outside on the pavement terrace, in the lobby-seating area or deeper inside the mirror-and-parquet-floor-lined interior. The design is contemporary but nods to Spanish tradition with bunches of dried dark red chillies and garlic bulbs strung up; the traditional hams hang by the bar. Once seated, warm bread in a basket and slices of Manchego cheese arrive (note, these aren't free tapas and will appear on your bill) so you can graze while you choose hot or cold tapas, from gazpacho Andaluz served in a glass to grilled artichoke flowers with olive oil. Boiled eggs stuffed with tuna and topped with mayonnaise

and chopped egg yolk make a rich but small-scale snack but the freshly fried plate of cod fritters (buñuelos cremosos de bacalao) are the best – break the crispy shell to reveal the creamy and, yes, dreamy centre. Toilets aren't generally something worth mentioning but the open-plan, open-brick downstairs loos here channel a New York club more than a Spanish bar. Worth checking out.

Calle de Alcalá, 19, 28014, grupocarbon.es

Casa Labra

Don't believe that Spaniards won't queue. Even at midweek lunchtimes, the line of locals lining up for a table at the restaurant or to stand at the bar of this stalwart close to Sol is 20-strong as it may well have been when it opened in 1860. It will get longer at the weekend. The terrace, really just the wide swerve of street outside the curved facade, has 1980s-style chrome tables and chairs; inside it's all very traditional with polished dark wood, marble-topped tables and blue and white tiles. The food is similarly old school – you're here, like everyone else, for the freshly fried fingers of crispy cod (at Casa Labra, they're known as tajadas de bacalao) or creamy croquettes that are the staple of Madrid tapas bars, despite the city being over 300 kilometres from the coastline. Older well-groomed male waiters dressed in the smart uniform of cropped starchy white jackets add a sense of ceremony. Colourful tiles and a chandelier liven up the dark interior, polished dark wood, and there's a restaurant if you don't want a fast turnaround. Fun fact: the Spanish Socialist Workers' Party (PSOE) was founded here in 1879 (a plaque reminds us). And yes, it was also a firm favourite of Ernest Hemingway.

Calle de Tetuán, 12, 28013, casalabra.es

Lhardy

The name may not sound Spanish, because it's French, but the food at this delicatessen-cum-café steps from Puerta de Sol is traditional Spanish to a T. In the ground-floor deli space order perfect ham croquettes, freshly made with puchero, the leftover bits and pieces from their cocido (chickpea, vegetable and meat stew), Madrid's famous broth-like soup (caldo del cocido) served in dainty white china bowls. Try the bocata de calamares, served hot-dog style in a paper boat, this is a soft white finger bun stuffed with fried battered calamari on grey-black squid ink mayonnaise. Everything is elegant here. Thirsty? Pour yourself a glass of chilled water from the antique silver urn. There is nothing as modern as a paper napkin here, only immaculately ironed and starched

Even the humble croquette is served on fine china at Lhardy

monogrammed linens. The motherly women who work here seem to enjoy recommending the celebration-style cakes, created with pleasing amounts of cream, puff pastry and chocolate, as if it were their own kitchen. Upstairs, there's a fine-dining restaurant for those who want to eat mainly French food in what is considered Madrid's first luxury restaurant, which opened in 1839. There's a top-hatted doorman, which certainly sets it apart from your average city bar.

Carrera de San Jerónimo, 8, 28014, lhardy.com

Casa de Comida D Diego

This is a charming example of a neighbourhood bar on the corner of Calle De León and Calle del Infante in the beating heart of the Barrio de las Letras. At the entrance, tables and chairs are set on monochrome tiles with shelves of plants trailing down from above. The long bar almost runs the length of the whitewashed brick interiors, topped with plants and a box of colourful citrus fruit. When you stop admiring the decor, tuck into orders of tapas that have just as much trouble taken with presentation as the decor. Yes, to Padrón peppers, some hot, some not, and freshly fried crisps – just like they used to make in British schools,

Right and overleaf: *Casa de Comida D Diego*

but these are less greasy. Also try sardines served on a bed of tomato pulp dotted with green olives and hard-boiled eggs in a creamy mayonnaise, the yellow yolk grated on top like cheese.

Calle León, 8, 28012, casadediegoleon.es

La Tia Cebolla

This unassuming corner bar with a blue painted ceiling and terracotta tiled floor isn't fancy but the service is good. There's a television in the corner showing sports with the sound down of course, while energising Latin tunes fills the space. It makes a change from the slicker, more tourist-tailored places on the jewel in the crown of the Barrio de las Letras, the Plaza Santa Ana, which is just around the corner. Prices are also far lower here than in many other similarly central bars. Tapas on the house include migas de pan – hot fried bread dusted with cumin – and the menu is big on traditional favourites such as solid wedges of tortilla. Beware, the heavy-handed salt distribution, with huge rocks scattered over piles of fried bottle-green Padrón peppers. Also try Argentinian empanadas (meat-filled turnovers) and the paella.

Calle de la Cruz, 27, 28012.

Tapas on the house at La Tia Cebolla

Lateral

One of a small group of homegrown tapas restaurants in Madrid and around the country, including Barcelona, Valencia and Málaga, this slender sophisticated bar suits the Plaza Santa Ana surroundings. Inside, the modern space is decorated in light wood and multiple pieces of art by contemporary artists, including Nobuyosi Araki, Doug Aitken and Candida Höfer, from sculptures to paintings. However, the terrace in the main square is the best place to be, particularly on one of Madrid's long summer nights when the lamps illuminate the terrace and

Above and opposite: *Fusion-style pinchos at Lateral*

water misters cool the air. Here you can take your time choosing from a menu that mixes classics such as tortilla de patatas and croquettes with internationally inspired fusion-style pinchos such as smoked salmon filled with a creamy yet refreshing blend of mascarpone, apple and salty ham served on toast. As you'd expect from the decor, the presentation is impeccable.

Plaza Santa Ana, 12, 28012, lateral.com

Restaurante Ginger

The smart blue awnings, art deco lamps and potted plant-clad exterior hints at the elegant interiors and there's an appealing vintage, stepped-back-in-time, look and feel to this glamorous restaurant with chequered and herringbone parquet floors, fabric covered banquette seating, clubby leather chairs and plenty of ornate mirrors. Aside from the floor-to-ceiling iron pillars, you'd never guess it was

Glamorous interiors and global small plates at Ginger

once a warehouse. The menu features plenty of types of gin and mojitos, and although it's not a traditional tapas restaurant, includes Padrón peppers and Iberian ham croquettes before sweeping across the globe from Spain to South and Central America. And so you'll find a small blue and white ceramic bowl of guacamole studded with red onion, fresh tomato and juicy sweetcorn kernels served with a wedge of lime, Mexican tortillas and a wooden pestle. Also order the crunchy green salad of fresh sprouts, thinly sliced carrots, curled courgettes, Portobello mushrooms and radishes. The latter isn't a bad thing, as a dose of

fresh raw veg balances all the fried food you're no doubt consuming in Madrid.

Plaza del Ángel, 12, 28012, andilana.com/locales/ginger

Cervecería Alemana

Famed Spain aficionado and legendary booze-fuelled writer Ernest Hemingway stayed drinking late into the night at this turn-of-the-century bar-restaurant on the café-lined Plaza de Santa Ana. Created by German industrialists to promote beer drinking, which morphed from selling beer only to adding tapas dishes to the menu, this Spanish take on a beer hall was also a crowd-pleaser with the generations of bullfighters who used to stay at the former Grand Hotel Reina Victoria – now the gleaming ME Madrid Reina Victoria visible across the square. Inside, the decor is pretty much unchanged. Inside, it's a simple arrangement of a long tapas-laden bar, dark wood panelling halfway up the walls and marble-topped tables with curved back chairs; Hemingway's is reserved in the right-hand corner – he chose a table by the window to enjoy the views of the square (although he also focused on beautiful women). It's old school in every way, meaning smart, white-jacketed waiters with black bow ties serve raciones of cured jamón Ibérico, albondigas (pork meatballs in sauce), and tripe, helped by a steady flow of

Hemingway's favourite,
Cervecería Alemana

cold draft lagers. If you come to the Barrio de las Letras, be sure to pop in.

Plaza de Santa Ana, 6, 28012, cerveceriaalemana.com

Cervecería El Diario

The clue is in the name. El diario means daily newspaper and this fun-filled bar in the heart of the Barrio de las Letras, dating back to 1897, has ceilings covered in faded old newspaper pages – and fans for the stifling summer months. Ironically the *El Diario* newspaper itself is now a popular digital platform, hidden behind a paywall and you can't paper a ceiling with a paywall, lending this something of a museum-like status. The long curving marble bar where art deco style lamps hang low is the place to graze on the authentic tapas dishes displayed in glass cases such as pulpo a la gallega (Galician-style octopus), anchovies in vinegar and tortilla de patatas. Order a glass of beer or vermouth and you'll receive a plate of tortilla cut into chunky squares and stubby breadsticks smothered in a thick brava-like sauce.

Calle de las Huertas, 69, 28014.

La Venencia

It could be said there isn't a bar in Madrid that old Ernest Hemingway or 'Papa Ernesto,' as he is known in Spain, didn't frequent, but this one is said to be a particular favourite of his or, to put it another way, he was the bar's most famous regular. He loved Spain but was obsessed with Madrid. The interior is pretty much as it was when he would have visited during the 1920s, and the anti-fascists gathered here during the Spanish Civil War in the 1930s. There's a strict no-photo, no-reservation policy, and the defiantly old-school attitude extends to the cobwebs left to cling to the barrels, the never-fading musty smell and the grumpiness of certain staff members. We forgive it all for the variety of dry Spanish sherries – Manzanilla, Fino, Oloroso, Amontillado and Palo Cortado – that are a far cry from an English granny's typical Christmas tipple. This bar is the main place in Madrid to come for a glass of Jerez. With the sherry, comes a variety of cold tapas – slices of fat-lined chorizo, pale triangles of Manchego cheese and fried almonds come free with each drink. Juicy bottle-green olives tend to be offered first. Orders are scribbled down in chalk; the battered metal cash register is equally old-school and all part of the rough charm. This is a place to obey and accept the rules and norms; do that, and you'll be allowed to come back again and again until the faded sherry posters, dusty bottles behind the bar and shabby decor begin to feel like home.

Calle de Echegaray, 7, 28014, lavenencia.com

La Abacería del Príncipe

Walking past what the owners refer to as an 'urban market', you'll see a deli-style glass case full of Spanish hams and thick wedges of cheese. Spain has at least 26 cheeses with a Protected Designation of Origin and many of them are to be found here. If that doesn't turn your head, the name – The Prince's Grocery – should prepare you for the wealth of food and drink that line the walls inside. Enter, and you find it's also a bar and wine merchant, with a corner spot for tasting the many wine labels on display in racks; move over to the high tables with stools, or you can sit at the long metal bar with a glass of Tio Pepe sherry and a board of sweet jamón with warm bread topped with pulped tomato. Shelves are well stocked with colourful jars of preserved olives, peppers and anchovies, which make gourmet gifts to take home if you're not a fan of the usual fridge magnet. A mixed-bag of music plays pub-style tunes and the staff are easy to get along with. It's also an easy place to sit on your own as the staff chat to you and keep your drink topped up, despite the busy central location a couple of blocks away from Sol.

Calle del Príncipe, 18, 28012.

Dani Moreno

Professional Chef and Cooking Teacher at Devour Tours.

From a very young age, food was my passion. I was lucky enough to

Dani Moreno

be born into a family with a strong tradition of cooking and eating well. I began learning the basics of the Mediterranean diet from the age of five. By then I had already helped make my first Spanish omelette and planted my first seeds in my grandfather's garden. He was a man closely related to the farming sector in Spain and was passionate about Mediterranean food.

I trained at the Casa de Campo Hospitality School in Madrid, then started my career in a small restaurant on the north coast of Spain. I have worked in some amazing hotels in Madrid including the Mandarin Oriental Ritz, Nodo with Alberto Chicote, Lakasa with César Martín and the Paradis Group.

Like my grandfather, I am passionate about helping people benefit from the Mediterranean diet, leading healthier and happier lives through the cuisine of my culture.

His five favourite tapas bars in Madrid are:

Casa Macareno – a wonderful example of how the past and future can coexist in one beautifully tiled place. Experience the simplicity and authentic atmosphere of a Spanish bar. Order patatas bravas, a reinterpretation of a classic Spanish dish, enhanced with new techniques.

El Montero de Cazorla Restaurant – this authentic corner of Andalusia in the centre of Madrid offers a southern atmosphere and fish and seafood menu that is highly regarded. The off-menu rice and fish are particularly popular.

Bar Melos – here you can find not only the largest and creamiest croquettes in Madrid, but also a wonderful example of two generations working together harmoniously.

Bar Malos – the owners of Bar Melos retired and passed the baton to a group of young entrepreneurs who opened a second bar in the heart of Malasaña. The concept and recipes remain, but the environment is bold, unconventional and appealing.

Ciriaco House – one of the oldest restaurants in Madrid has a rich history reflected in its walls and cellars. The wine collection is particularly noteworthy, featuring vintages that span over a century. Order the piquillo pepper tapa stuffed with chicken.

His favourite recipe is Lydia's alioli:

I'm particularly fond of my mother's alioli recipe, which is straightforward yet incredibly flavoursome. It is a versatile sauce that pairs well with fish and vegetables, or as a dip, and most importantly, it is a wonderful complement to the authentic Valencian paella. Here's how she makes it:

Add egg yolk, garlic, salt and vinegar (or lemon) to a tall glass or cup. Ideally use a hand blender, adding oil and blend until the mixtures become thick and creamy. Gradually add in the rest of the oil. Move the blender up and down to fluff the mixture, with slow, gentle movements. If the aioli is becoming too thick or the oil begins to separate, may add a few drops of cold water and continue to blend.

1 egg yolk
1 clove of garlic
1 tsp salt (to taste)
1 teaspoon vinegar or lemon juice
230ml sunflower or olive oil
    (not extra virgin)

5

LA LATINA, LAVAPIÉS & MADRID RÍO-ARGANZUELA

One of the oldest neighbourhoods in Madrid, and once the Muslim quarter, La Latina is a traditionally working-class area with slender medieval lanes leading to sun-filled squares and a restaurant featured in the Guinness World Records. Sobrino de Botín, the oldest continually open restaurant in the world, has been livening up the Calle de Cuchilleros since 1725, with a museum-like interior virtually unchanged and a wood-burning oven

La Latina is a lively barrio of narrow lanes lined with tapas bars (Veronica H on Unsplash)

said to have never gone out (although it's unlikely anyone could disprove this claim). Fun fact: the Romantic Spanish painter Goya worked here as a waiter and, no prizes for guessing, it was a favourite of Ernest Hemingway who fed his stomach with roasted suckling pig and the pages of his novel, *The Sun Also Rises*, with a scene set here describing the restaurant's most prized dish.

A five-minute walk southwest of Plaza Mayor, La Latina is known as Madrid's best tapas neighbourhood, with the stretch between the parallel streets of Cava Baja and Cava Alta lined with around 50 bars and restaurants.

If you need a sit down after all that bouncing from bar to bar, the eighteenth-century Príncipe de Anglona Garden is an understated sweet spot adjacent to the palace. Thanks to the tall walls surrounding it on one side of the Plaza de la Paja, the brick-pathed garden goes largely unnoticed.

What cannot go unnoticed is the Segovia Viaduct, which arches high above Calle de Segovia. Built to connect this older side of the city with the Royal Palace, this photogenic stack of granite is a famous local landmark and makes appearances in Spanish filmmaker Pedro Almodóvar's

The Castilian Dining Room at the famous Sobrino de Botín

films. At once a good-looking architectural marvel and a sadder site of suicides since it was built (once in 1874, out of iron and wood and again in 1934, out of concrete), until tall acrylic screens were put up in the 1980s.

Hard to miss on the Plaza de la Cebada, the stadium-sized Mercado de la Cebada still sets out its stalls underneath the colourful domes as a local-focused fruit, veg, fish and meat-for-all market yet the elements that have changed other neighbourhood markets are slowly creeping in. El Rastro, Madrid's Sunday morning flea market, is as much a weekend ritual as going to church and brings thousands to the stalls sprawling along the Calle de la Ribera de Curtidores, and by extension the many bars in the area. Expect to find anything from new and second-hand clothes, antique furniture to rare vinyl.

With a higher concentration of immigrants than any other neighbourhood in Madrid, Lavapiés has a diverse community whose mixed cultural heritage is reflected in its bars, restaurants and shops. This working-class neighbourhood south-east of the city centre has become home to migrants moving in from the

El Rastro market

rural areas, a pattern repeated by the Ecuadorians, Colombians, Moroccans, Africans, Chinese and Bangladeshis who make up the multicultural population here.

Of course there's a local market, and the Antón Martín is easy to spot, on the borders of Lavapiés and Barrio de las Letras, painted a rich shade of terracotta with an arresting mural of a tattooed woman on one side by artist Fin Dac. This attractive building has the typical food market atmosphere and all the cheese, fish, fruit and veg you'd expect, and a few bars reflecting the area's multicultural and regional heritage.

Each autumn, Tapapiés tapas festival ramps up the focus on affordable tapas for all, a self-guided tapas tour of the area's bars and restaurants which offer tapas for a few euros during the last two weeks in October.

Spooning around La Latina and Lavapiés and bordering Atocha, Madrid Río is a riverside redevelopment that's part of the wider re-greening of Madrid. While tourists tend to congregate around the more obvious landmarks, locals enjoy the uncrowded swathe of greenery that hugs the Casa de Campo.

In multicultural Lavapiés you'll find everything from traditional tapas to global versions

Antón Martín food market in colourful Lavapiés

created urban biodiversity that includes the return of wildlife not seen in the city for decades including endangered otters.

As far from the beaches that bring millions of tourists to Spain as it's possible to be, Madrid has gained an urban beach of sorts, which is the cherry on the top for the sporty families who inhabit the city's green lung.

Also, by the river, Matadero Madrid is a red brick neo-Mudejar encased slaughterhouse reborn as a massive cultural complex housing rotating art exhibitions, film screenings, plays and live music. And of course, there's a tapas bar.

Read on for a selection of places to eat for tapas lovers.

This once neglected area of the city was wrapped around an ugly ring road, the M-30, cutting off the locals' access to the polluted Rio Manzanares that ran alongside it. In an unusual move, the M-30 was buried underneath a park and topped with trees running along the riverbank. Reconnecting the city to the river has

Museo de La Empanada, Mercado de la Cebada

If your feet are dragging after a day's sightseeing or perhaps you've overdone the vermouth on tap the night before, a visit to this small bar on the first floor of the Mercado de la Cebada will pep you up. The Columbian owner is an engaging man who runs his

Museo de la Empanada in Mercado de la Cebada

business well, embracing social media (he's all over TikTok) and running a mini empanada empire. Selling the empanadas in the name, tamales and all manner of South American street food dishes, the arepas are the thing, corn flatbreads filled with cheese (choclo) or vegan, filled with cumin-flavoured kidney beans, onions and tomato. You think there's nowhere to sit and you'll find yourself a bench on the square outside, then he pulls up a metal stool so you can eat in. There's an actual restaurant way out of central Madrid, should you find yourself in Carabanchel.

Plaza de La Cebada, 28005.

Taberna el Tempranillo

On the bar-lined Cava Baja Street, in one of the city's most popular tapas areas, La Latina, this bar-restaurant launched in the 90s is all things to everyone. That it's all about wines is clear from the racks that stretch up across an entire wall, from almost all regions of Spain (the place is named after the variety

Taberna el Tempranillo in La Latina

of grape). The rest of the space is bare brick or faded yellowish painted walls, with yet more wine bottles propped on available spaces such as shelves halfway up walls. It's a place for families to dine on a handful of high-quality Castilian specialities at the few tables arranged under the rustic beams, or equally to come alone and sit at the wooden bar, so long it turns midway, with a glass of wine (weekly changing wines by the glass will be recommended by the knowledgeable staff). As you do, delivery men wheel in boxes of wine or orders for vegetables, such as seasonal mushrooms they turn into a winning dish. Pincho de setas is a delight to eat, simply made from a wild chanterelle-like mushroom, cooked so it's smoky served on a rustic slab of artisanal bread smeared with creamy alioli. Although Spain is associated with macho meat dishes, such as beef cheek, pig's ear and cured ham, the country is home to around 1,500 species of wild mushrooms. Other specialities include chickpeas from Fuentesaúco sautéed with squid or grilled squid and artichoke. If you don't like wine, draft beer is also available.

Calle de la Cava Baja, 38, 28005.

Tiles and tapas at Taberna Salamanca

Taberna Salamanca

Also on Cava Baja, this tiny bar looks like a hole in the wall, less grand than neighbouring Casa Lucio, a long-standing wood-fronted restaurant which people queue to dine at and you need a reservation even just to sit at the bar. In contrast, this little place is down to earth with a teeny bar as you enter and small dining space behind and upstairs lined with terracotta tiles on the floor, more halfway up the walls and a wall-hung television failing to be low key in a wooden frame. The menu is equally traditional, with morcilla de Burgos and croquettes on the menu. The queso curado (sheep's milk cheese) comes neatly arranged with a drizzle of olive oil among a menu of similarly well priced items such as patatas bravas and Russian salad. The staff are welcoming, multi-lingual, advise on which wine to drink and generally make you feel at ease in one of the most popular areas for nightlife in Madrid.

Calle de la Cava Baja, 31, 28005.

Cañas y Tapas

Sometimes it's easy to be snobby about certain types of chain restaurants, but this one deserves a bit more respect. One of over 10 in the city, the branch in La Latina is a freshly painted whitewashed space, which is a nice contrast to the gamut of woodsy places where, yes, some of the best tapas are to be had, among the dusty bottles and creaky beams. Here, you can order the tapas you'd order anywhere else, from Padrón peppers sautéed with olive oil and tossed in sea salt flakes, patatas bravas with alioli, Spanish omelette and fried aubergine, cooling bowl of gazpacho, served with chopped green pepper lending a picante flavour, (the croutons can be left), or fed to the pigeons pecking around the Plaza del Humilladero. More typical fast-food menu items are also here, from chicken wings to burgers, and regional ones too,

Trad tapas and fast food at Cañas y Tapas

such as Asturian cachopo (breaded veal stuffed with ham and melted cheese).

Plaza del Humilladero, 4, 28005, canasytapas.es

Bar Cruz – Casa De Las Navajas

If you thought laminated photos of the dishes served were something reserved for tourist traps only, think again. There's an entire wall with photos of pretty much every dish this La Latina bar serves, which is useful, let's not be snobbish. This bar is clear about a few things – it's not here to win any prizes for interior design – nor exterior, which resembles slices of chorizo – nor for service. But it does so with a certain charm. A sign above the bar clearly states 'There's no Wi-Fi but you can speak to us. We don't speak English (most of us), but we promise not to laugh at your Spanish.' But the food is good. Really good. Seafood spans razor clams – the navajas in the name to zamburiñas (small scallops); snails in a rich tomato sauce sit in the glass case at eye level if you sit at the bar. If that's not your thing and your blood pressure is low, go for the Padrón peppers (be warned, the salt level is high) and patatas bravas in the typical spicy sauce.

Calle de las Maldonadas, 1, 28005, casadelasnavajas.com

Below and overleaf: *Fresh seafood and vegetarian tapas at Bar Cruz*

Los Caracoles (Casa Amadeo Los Caracoles)

Don't be put off by the name of this legendary bar on the edge of Lavapiés and La Latina. Yes, caracoles mean snails in Spanish, and they are the speciality, with around 20 kilos cradled in the house spicy sauce cooked with added chorizo sold each day. However, the menu runs from seafood to the firmly vegetarian judías viudas and tortilla. The gazpacho is perfect, served in a traditional terracotta bowl with tiny containers filled with chopped peppers, onion and tomato. Known colloquially as Los Caracoles, the slither of a bar is usually standing room only, with a narrow space widening into an L-shape to the rear where there's a table and stools (right by the toilet). After the Rastro, it naturally packs out with bargain-lovers enjoying the high quality dishes Burgo-born owner Amadeo Lázaro, father of seven, has been churning out since the 1940s, including Burgos blood sausage, tripe and battered cod.

Plaza de Cascorro, 106, 28005, caracolesdeamadeo.com

Los Caracoles specialises in snails and popular dishes such as gazpacho

El Madroño

This cheerful combination of red painted wooden exterior and traditional tiles depicting scenes of jolly people eating and drinking in the 'olden days' no doubt attracts tourists to this tavern on the border of La Latina and Las Austrias (which is part of a group of three in Madrid). Once inside, history boffins can peruse the tiled explanation of the city's coat of arms and how it has changed over the years. The name is all about the symbol of the city, that big furry brown bear pawing the strawberry bush sculpture you've no doubt walked past in Puerta del Sol. If you're here for the marcha – a lively time – stand at the long wooden bar and knock back a shot of the strawberries-meet-sloe-gin-like specialty house liqueur served in an edible chocolate-lined wafer cup or chupito, called El Oso y El Madroño. If you're here for the food, order slices of morcilla (black pudding), Russian salad and moreish grandma's-style meatballs.

Plaza de Puerta Cerrada, 7, 28005, grupoelmadrono.com/en/

Tal Qual, Antón Martín Market

Among the stalls of fresh fish, meat, fruit and vegetables, including specialities such as olives – Spain has something like 200 varieties – from lunchtime onwards, bars and restaurants start to open up at the Antón Martín Market. Señoras and abuelas local to Lavapiés come to shop for dinner among the three floors of high-quality food and drink including traditional Argentine empanadas and Asian noodles. If you get lost and head up to the top floor, you'll find the Amor de Dios flamenco dance school. In the far back corner on the first floor, Tal Qual is a family-run spot with just a couple of tables and chairs, but this doesn't stop customers crowding in for the homestyle croquetas caseras filled with good things, from cheese to mushrooms, and plates of thinly sliced jamón.

Calle de Santa Isabel, 528012, mercadoantonmartin.com

Los Chuchis

With a prime location in the heart of multicultural Lavapiés on Calle del Amparo, this cheerful café bar represents something different, not just for the area but for Madrid. Chuchi's is owned by Scott Preston, a white-bearded Brit, whose eclectic collections displayed on shelves reveal his heritage, from China teapots to a box of Scott's porage oats and royal coronation memorabilia, such as a 1953 scrapbook. The interior looks – and feels – like a homely checked tiled floor kitchen full of cookery books and

Below and opposite: *Cheerful café-bar Los Chuchis*

bottles of wine. The rich bluey-green painted woodwork, outside and in, brings to mind Mediterranean islands, while the menu includes firmly British staples such as sausages with mustard and shepherd's pie, but also raciones such as potato skins – gnarly and crispy, as they should be – with the winning combination of cooling sour cream and a spicy tomato-based sauce. There's something good here for everyone.

Calle del Amparo, 82, Centro, 28012.

Lamiak

Sister to the La Latina original which was a meeting place for the arty types involved in the Movida Madrileña during the 1980s, this Lavapiés bar focuses firmly on Basque food. The house specialties are pinchos – pintxos in the Basque language – made to order in a steady stream flowing from the kitchen, from creamy goat cheese topped with tomato and sweet caramelised onion to the heady mix of rich brie and smoked salmon, all served on tiny slates. You'll find locals and tourists sitting at the well-scrubbed wooden bar or on tiny stalls at tables among the exposed brick walls and jazz festival posters drinking wine, beer and cocktails. Even on a weekday night it's full by 8pm. Some say the staff are friendly; some say rude. In reality, it probably depends on the day but if you struggle with Spanish they speak good English.

Calle de la Rosa 10, 28012.

El Automático

On the main street for bars in Lavapiés, Calle de Argumosa, where Tapapiés takes place, this unassuming bar is known for its generous portions and welcoming staff. Inside there are mis-matched groups of tables, bar stools and chairs, some wooden, some painted metal, or you can sit at a long wooden bar and appreciate the freebies – slices of chorizo, cheese and doll-sized dishes of pisto dished up under your nose. Mainly rock music blares out (if you don't like U2, sit outside where there's a couple of tables and chairs on the street). For meat-eaters, the meatballs – tasty tennis ball sized and come top and tailed with fried potatoes – are good value and a meal in themselves. If you're lucky, the genial owner will offer you a little liqueur in a miniature glass 'on the house' as you leave. And if that isn't enough incentive to return, then what is?

Calle de Argumosa, 17, 28012.

La Mancha

This Lavapiés staple packs out at the weekend, probably for the swift, smiley service and the well-plated up, good quality tapas. Old men, young couples, everyone comes. Even dogs are welcome. Decor-wise, it's simple with a long marble bar and terracotta tiled floor; extra seats are available outside. There are also two doors side by side (one for entering, one for leaving?). But the truth is you're not here for the

La Mancha in lively Lavapiés

interior design. Order a drink and get some complimentary chorizo slices with stubby breadsticks then tuck into the menu of raciones, which include staples such as slim-cut triangles of cream-coloured Manchego cheese with rich and oily sun-dried tomatoes and a plate of deep red, thinly sliced mojama with a scattering of toasted almonds on top.

Calle Miguel Servet, 13, 28012.

Taberna Alabanda

This popular local haunt in Lavapiés is the headquarters for Madrid´s blues society, and regular live music seems just one of many draws. Regulars and newcomers come for the easy-going vibe and the free montaditos, which include made-to-order squares of perfect tortilla placed on slices of bread and delivered with your beer or wine. It's a scruffy space with a dilapidated old barrel outside and a mishmash of chairs inside, as well as on the street, but it's part of the local furniture and will no doubt be here in decades to come. Perhaps one day people will talk about it as they do the places frequented by Hemingway decades ago.

Calle de Miguel Servet, 15, 28012.

Atrapallada

If you've overdone the traditional old-style bars a bit and are yearning for a light and modern setting for your tapas, Atrapallada is a space an

architect clearly took time to dream up (and draw up). Chunky concrete pillars are dressed in clean vertical lengths of rope (a nod to the windswept sea their speciality seafood comes from), and also divide spaces, while open shelving and well-placed furniture creates different zones. A simple decor of light wood (oak) and a soft grey colour palette – sometimes blue – including octagonal tiles and striped aprons, creates a place you want to sit in by large paneless windows and try their Galician seafood such as pulpo a la gallega or truffle-laced tortilla de patatas made for one. This being Spain, there's still a leg of ham on the side for carving. The one concession to cosy is the dark Chesterfield sofa at the far end, where you can also curl up with

Below and opposite: *Atrapallada*

a book and one of their popular mini hamburguesas. There's also a glass-fronted terrace outside. The best bit is the welcoming staff offers take away, which is perfect if you're staying close to where Lavapiés meets the Madrid Río/Arganzuela district, and where the city becomes more suburban, residential and therefore less touristy.

Paseo de las Acacias, 12, 28005, restauranteatrapallada.com/

Enrique Tomás, Atocha Station

Stations can often be seedy places, but Madrid Atocha, the biggest railway station in Spain and the first to be built in the capital, is home to a very special place to sit and wait for your train. The

Opposite and above: *Enrique Tomás in the plant-filled Atocha station*

original arched train shed that opened in 1892 no longer has tracks; Rafael Moneo, the same architect who revamped the nearby Prado Museum, created the greenhouse-style 4,000-square-metre tropical garden with more than 7,200 plants growing under the natural light, including banana, coconut and breadfruit trees. Once there were turtles living in a pond, but they had to be relocated due to naughty locals dumping their unwanted fish here. Shops and restaurants on the ground floor concourse include a branch of Enrique Tomás, a pretty good chiringuito-style deli-slash-tapas bar dishing out walnut-topped goat's cheese salads in full view of the garden. Strings of lights and bottles of Mahou beer serve as bunting-like decoration while leafy plants reference the nearby greenery. You can also pick up a packet of jamón Ibérico or a pack of cured sheep's cheese from the deli area to stash in your case if you're hopping on a train somewhere.

Calle Estación Atocha, Calle de Méndez Álvaro, 28045, enriquetomas.com

Bodegas Rosell

On the corner of Calle General de Lacy and Calle de las Delicias – the latter street name is an apt clue to the delicious

QUE RICO VINO
VALDEPEÑAS
EXQUISITO
VERMOUTH

BODEGAS ROSELL
14
VINOS DE JEREZ Y RIOJA
EY

Opposite and above: *Sample authentic tapas dishes at Bodegas Rosell*

dishes served at this royal, blue-painted corner barrio bar right around the corner from the plant-filled Atocha train station. Despite the location, you won't find many tourists here and don't expect service with a smile – as in so many Madrid bars, it tends to be brusque and functional. You will be smiling, however, when the busy waiters in burgundy shirts whisk plates of salted crisps and mussels to pick at with wooden toothpicks while you wait for your generous portion of cod steeped in garlic and olive oil and aubergine with a creamy tomato sauce.

Inside, it's as traditional as can be, with guitars hung on walls, barrels set with stools and wooden tables dressed in smart white cloths. The Rosell family converted a former wine shop into a bar in 1920, as the tiles on the front indicate, which were painted by Alfonso Romero, who also painted parts of the Plaza de Toros de las Ventas (the most famous bullring in Madrid). Wines by the glass change every month.

Calle General Lacy 14, 28045, bodegasrosell.es

Jorge Sigüenza

Head Chef at The Level Bar, Generator Madrid.

Originally from Ecuador, Head Chef Jorge Sigüenza fell in love with cooking when he moved to Madrid at the age of 18, charmed by the local food scene. He began his career working in various bars and restaurants – Colonia Sacramento, Pizzería Emporio and Taberna del Alabardero – including his own family bar and restaurant. Jorge is also passionate about art and paints in his spare time.

Jorge Sigüenza

His five favourite tapas bars in Madrid are:

El Tigre – famous for its generous free tapas with every drink.

Casa Labra – a historical classic known for its cod croquettes.

La Ardosa – a traditional tapas bar with an excellent selection of vermouths and tapas.

Bodega de la Ardosa – perfect for enjoying Spanish omelette and other delicacies.

El Sur – popular for its creative tapas and cosy atmosphere.

His favourite recipe is:

A recipe I always enjoy with family is braised oxtail. Requiring meticulous preparation and slow cooking, this dish is a gem of traditional cuisine. The meat, slow cooked with red wine, vegetables, and spices, becomes tender and full of flavour. Every step, from searing the meat to reducing the sauce, requires patience and dedication, ensuring an explosion of flavours in every bite.

Wash and dry the pieces of oxtail well. Season with salt and pepper and lightly flour. Brown the oxtail in a large pan with a good splash of olive oil, then remove and set aside. In the same pan, add a little more oil if necessary, and sauté the onion, garlic, leek, peppers, carrot and celery until tender and lightly browned.

Add the chopped tomatoes and cook until they form a sauce. Deglaze the pan by pouring in the red wine and cooking over high heat until the liquid reduces.

Return the oxtail to the pan. Add the beef stock, bay leaves, thyme and rosemary. Make sure the liquid covers the meat well (you can add more stock or water if necessary). Bring to the boil, lower the heat and cover. Simmer for around three hours, stirring occasionally, until the meat is tender and separates easily from the bone.

5 kg of oxtail, cut into pieces
2 large onions, chopped
3 carrots, sliced
2 ripe tomatoes, peeled and chopped
1 red pepper, chopped
1 green pepper, chopped
4 cloves garlic, chopped
1 leek, sliced
1 celery stalk, sliced
1 glass red wine
1 glass of beef stock
2 bay leaves
1 sprig thyme

6

MARKETS

It's a sentiment touched on elsewhere in this book, but one worth repeating. For many of us, markets are the lifeblood of a city and nosing around them is by far the best way to achieve that hackneyed old cliché of getting under its skin. The produce you can buy in them, and the sellers and food stalls you'll find in them, tell you a lot about the neighbourhood they are in as well as about the city. If the palaces and parks in the capital city, each with their own beauty, are the heart, Madrid's markets, which reflect its bars and restaurants in that they offer regional produce as well as increasingly international, are the soul.

For Madrid, a city with such a diverse number of districts, each with its particular character, markets represent the people who live close by them, who shop in them and the socio-economic changes happening in and around them. These elements evolve, shifting with immigration and investment, among other factors. It may sound like a trite tourist board slogan, but to know Madrid's markets is to know Madrid.

Some centuries-old markets have been made over and upgraded by installing Michelin-star chefs selling glossy dishes attracting tourists aplenty and displaying fruit and veg in architectural ways, while others remain as they always have been, places for the home cook to buy their ingredients and for home-style chefs and cooks to sell their tortillas and tripe among a familiar, loyal and receptive community.

Madrid has around 50 markets, which isn't surprising for a city so food focused.

Here is a selection of some of the most famous and worth visiting.

Mercado de San Miguel

For market purists, who prefer a more down-to-earth space full of the usual piles of fruit, veg and a few low-key food stalls, the Mercado de San Miguel is just too glamorous, too touristy and too expensive. You can see their point and with over seven million visitors per year it now draws more than the Goya-filled Prado museum. However, in fairness, you can find tapas for €1 and the odd local has been known to pop in for an aperitivo. Not to mention

Above, below and overleaf pages: *Over seven million people visit Mercado de San Miguel each year*

skewered with skinny green guindilla peppers, pieces of cheese and tomatoes, some steeped in flecks of herbs. Then there are the bowls of patatas bravas and curvaceous chunks of crackling; neat rows of seafood skewers, others lined with chargrilled Padrón peppers, rounds of black pudding or juicy aubergine.

Fancy a shot of cooling gazpacho pimped with crab and decorated with delicate pea shoots? It's also here (find the tiny King Crab stall in the middle section) near Mr. Martin's fake printed newspaper cones of fritto misto; paellas made by Michelin-starred chef Rodrigo de la Calle and chocolate con churros all keep it firmly Spanish. As do Galician oysters on ice. Then there's the bars selling cooling glasses of pink Cava, rich red sangria and frothy little cañas.

But you'll also find fusion boat-like tacos filled with egg and prawns, chicken and pesto and big burgers. Kitsch lollipops and ice creams are sold at Rocambolesc, owned by three-Michelin-star chef Jordi Roca. With food and drink from so many regions, this is a good starting point if you're new to Spanish food. Go at night when the illuminated stalls are visible through the glass panels. The prices can be way higher here than Madrid's more traditional markets but think of it as a museum devoted to food if you don't feel like queuing for half a day to get into the Prado.

three-Michelin-starred chefs. It's also a bit of a looker, the original wrought-iron-and-glass structure – the only one in Spain – just off Plaza Mayor in Los Austrias beginning as a wholesale food market in 1916 before being smartened up over a six-year renovation, which finished in 2009. If you're not shy of crowds and noise – early evening feels like a big party – it's worth a visit for the sheer variety of stalls selling high quality produce and dishes from Madrid, Castilla, Asturias and the Basque Country (33 at the last count, but it seems like a lot more). Glass cases tease you with over 20 types of sheeny green olives, some

Plaza de San Miguel,
mercadodesanmiguel.es

Mercado de Antón Martín

Come before midday and you might think this market in the Lavapiés neighbourhood is operating at half-mast. Despite being a few minutes' walk from the tourist-filled Sol and Las Letras areas, it's an old timer's place for locals living in these very same areas to shop. Yes, you can buy speciality olives and glass dishes displaying cheap tapas you can take home, such as chicharrón y queso skewers (pork belly and cheese). The Queseria cheese shop sells dozens of types of Spanish and European cheeses including sheep and goat, mostly made from raw milk and from small farms – a useful poster shows the nation's best and which region they hail from – but also glasses of vermouth you can sip seated at their two or three tables. But the tapas bars and restaurants tend to be closed, wooden stools turned upside down on high tables and the metal shutters are firmly pulled down. Come a little later in the day, say for lunch, and the eat-in side of the market stirs into life.

Among the Japanese and Mexican bars serving sushi, ramen and guacamole, you'll find traditional and modern Spanish (Dopplegänger and Sincio). Stand at a marble-topped wooden barrel at the self-explanatory Tapas Y Vinos, for cheese and wine, while Tal Qual is a teeny corner bar producing hundreds of homemade croquetas caseras, filled with ham,

Tourist-free Mercado de Antón Martín

cheese and mushrooms, among the tapas and raciones. Spot Asian Army by its green and red lampshades, loved for its street-food-style southeast Asian dishes and the market itself for its paprika-coloured exterior decorated with a masked, tattooed woman above the main entrance on Calle de Santa Isabel (there are three different entrances). On the top floor there's a flamenco school and at street level, paving the way to the market, are butchers, fishmongers and the usual produce. All this is a block from the Metro stop of the same name – Antón Martín.

Calle de Santa Isabel, 5, 28012, mercadoantonmartin.com

Mercado de la Paz

Built in 1882, this is one of Madrid's oldest markets and despite its location in one of the city's poshest districts, it's one of the most down-to-earth. Surrounded by famous Madrid streets such as Serrano, Ortega y Gasset and Claudio Coello, the Mercado de la Paz in Salamanca is an art nouveau landmark designed by the same Eiffel who built a certain tower in Paris. Most markets reflect their local community, so you'd expect a grander-looking place to suit the well-heeled clientele who live among the expensive apartments and close to the Plaza Margaret Thatcher, which was

Casa Dani at Mercado de la Paz in Salamanca

opened a decade ago (this right-wing memorial wouldn't happen in an area such as Lavapiés). However, this is an unassuming neighbourhood market where stall owners who've worked here for generations know all the regulars who come in search of good quality ingredients for tonight's dinner, be it a jar of preserved Spanish anchovies or a bottle of homegrown wine. There's a mix of fresh fish, charcuterie and cheese stalls inside and out as well as deli-style shops selling specialty food products such as mojama (salt-cured tuna loin).

Among the places to eat tapas, Casa Dani is the most famous. It's a no-frills kind of place, with a daily-changing menu crowned by an onion-rich, oozey on the inside, Spanish omelette. Depending on your appetite, you can order it in three different portion sizes – pintxo, media ración and una ración. Many people consider this to be the best tortilla in Madrid, others the best in Spain, which would basically mean it was the best in the world, so eligible for being celebrated in the Guinness World Records if the researchers are interested. Regardless, it's worth trying whether you're in the area or making a special pilgrimage.

Calle de Ayala 28, mercadolapaz.es

Mercado de la Cebada

Taking up a sizable chunk of Plaza de la Cebada, Mercado de la Cebada's colourful façade is the biggest landmark in a neighbourhood famed for its variety of tapas bars. Two football-pitch-sized floors of what you'd expect from an 1875-born local market (rebuilt in the 1950s), meaning a no-frills array of stalls selling meat, fish, fruit and vegetables although it will no doubt gradually add in more of the type of bars that bring the tourists. It's no looker but the charm is in the produce and food stalls. Here you can try classic Madrileñan fare cooked as if someone's granny has laboured over it in her kitchen, such as croquettes, pig's ear, tortilla de patatas, black pudding, and more at more traditional stands like Bar Doña, helped down with as many cañas as you can manage. Or delicious Colombian empanadas filled with meat or beans for vegans and vegetarians.

What stands out among the boxes of ripe melons and shiny onions are the wonky non-spherical tomatoes, which are fittingly the size of footballs and make you vow never to eat a flavourless tiny cherry tomato ever again. Vendors know the appeal – signs warn if you touch, you pay. If so much fresh produce inspires you, try one of the cooking workshops held for adults and children, spanning cakes, sushi, roasts and hummus. There's also a variety of non-food stands, from bric-a-brac to clothing, handbags, books and art. On Saturday lunchtime, all of the market's seafood stalls convert into pop-up tapas bars – a tradition known as la mariscada, where you can sample prawns, octopus and mussels prepared as you wait.

Plaza de la Cebada, mercadodelacebada.com

Above and overleaf: *Mercado de la Cebada*

Mercado de Chamberí

There's an almost Truman Show-like feel to this pristine covered market with an immaculately tiled floor set back from the road near the Museo Sorolla in Chamberí, dedicated to Spain's most famous impressionist painter. Modern additions are the gym and swimming pool that top this 1940s-built structure and these days you can visit the website for a virtual tour before you even leave your house; you can even order online. However, it's still fairly traditional, known for the quality and the variety of the produce, from the giant spring onions, neon-yellow lemons and other produce that almost seem fake, so perfect and clean you can't believe they ever grew from the earth. Fresh pink prawns and spiky-shelled whelks rest on mounds of crushed ice; whole stalls are devoted to shiny green and black olives, freshly baked loaves of brown and white bread and multiple types of cheeses, all displayed with the same finesse. You can try slices of traditional Spanish hams from La Jamoneria de Juan or Jamonera Castellana or French cheese and wine from Brie Alto.

While still traditional, the market is moving with the times to include La Chispería, a food hall-style space to the rear which collates a few bars and restaurants where you can sit at high stalls or lower benches for eating Asturian tapas dishes such as chorizo with cider and cachopos (veal fillets with cheese and ham) at Cachopo & Go – they also serve croquettes. Juanchos BBQ's steaks and acorn-fed Iberian pork and De Queso's special cheesecake (tarta de queso), a baked-style creation with a caramelised top, are all on sale in this area of the market. Sports fans are encouraged to eat their favourite foods here without missing out on watching major games on the wall-mounted televisions. In a food and football-crazy city like Madrid, what more could you ask for? Begin or end your night here weaving in stops at the multiple bars around Calle Ponzano and Plaza de Olavide.

Calle de Alonso Cano 10, 28010, mercadodechamberi.es

Mercado de San Antón

This contemporary chunk of a building on a Chueca side street among the organic bakeries and tattoo shops houses three tiers of glamorously displayed food and drink. The concrete shopping centre-like exterior may not immediately appeal, although it has been designed to reference the area's residential façades, which add charm with their iron balconies hung with rainbow flags, but what's on sale inside no doubt will if you're here to eat. San Antón isn't a market for getting your shoes re-heeled or ferreting around for household items: it's a food hall on steroids. There's a pristine supermarket on the ground floor; the first floor sells meat and fish in stalls such as Octavio's delicatessen with over 300 types of cheese, ham and salmon; on the second, tapas bars include Taberna La Ancha, for Spanish omelettes, plus Greek and Japanese stalls; and on the third, an indoor-outdoor rooftop restaurant, the foliage-filled 11 Nudos Terraza Nordés, where locals gather for drinks after work, rewards the effort with views over the area's romantic rooftops. For many, the highlight of the market is this third-floor rooftop terrace with posh tapas given a special spin, from patatas a la brava to ensaladilla Atlántica to soak up the cocktails.

What you'll find here is very much a local market, with surprisingly far fewer tourists that visit the quainter-looking wrought iron and glass Mercado de San Miguel. This is a good thing, with fewer people meaning you can take your time dawdling over freshly fried croquettes on the first floor El Bar de San Antón or choosing which flavour artisan ice cream to order from the second-floor Mistura, including pistachios, coconut, hazelnuts or water-based with mango and grapefruit. Here, like in so many other Madrid markets now, you can sample Peruvian street food, from tamales to vegan ceviche (with mushrooms) in Ceviches & Wok. While the remodelling may not appeal to those who love vintage buildings, this is now far more of a sustainable market, with a central skylight acting as a huge photovoltaic energy collector and a floor made from recycled molten basalt.

Calle de Augusto Figueroa 24, 28004, mercadosananton.com

Mercado de San Ildefonso

This modern take on the traditional Spanish food market is housed in a prettified industrial space at the head of Calle Fuencarral, one of the biggest and busiest shopping streets in Madrid, where Chueca and Malasaña rub fun-loving shoulders. Metres from the site of the original, named after what once was Madrid's first covered market, since demolished in the 1970s, it's very East London in terms of architecture and design. Now you know to expect bare brickwork, metal beams and exposed pipes with plenty of concrete, wood, iron, steel and copper. The lighting is nice with neon bar signs and art deco lamps brought from Paris; there's also a very tall tree made from rope.

Like the Mercado de San Miguel, this is a food stall-only place, styled as a street food market with three floors of stalls with a bar on each, yet it feels less polished, more youth-orientated in many ways, like the bar-lined surrounding streets. Although it's not strictly speaking street food that you'll find here, instead more traditional Spanish tapas dishes from tortilla de patatas to ham-topped pinchos,

Above and overleaf: *Food stalls at Mercado de San Ildefonso*

Mexican tacos (the wonderfully rhyming Paco's Tacos) and Venezuelan tequeños (fried fingers of white cheese-stuffed pastry). Spanish foods are the mainstay, from La boutique del ibérico selling blistered, rock-salt drenched Padrón peppers in tin paella pans to the Jaleo croquetas bar selling 'grandmother's recipe' homemade croquettes stuffed with fillings that traverse the usual ham to include mushrooms, langoustine, truffle and Gorgonzola cheese. Pincholand naturally sells combinations of Spanish pinchos or tapas. Regardless of its mislabelling, it's a happening place to hang out, buy a beer and take your tapas to sit on one of the patios – one more wood-focused, the other more leafy – once your little buzzer lets you know your food is ready. The effect of the design and edited selection of stalls is to create a fun place to go for tapas, which is why it's always packed out.

Calle de Fuencarral 57, 28004, mercadodesanildefonso.com

Mercado de Los Mostenses

You'd expect a market this multicultural to be tucked away in one of Madrid's less central neighbourhoods. Yet stray just one block in from the tourist-thronged Gran Vía, at the Plaza de España end, and you'll find this low-key firmly neighbourhood market. Originally a grander market, built from iron and glass in the nineteenth century, it was demolished in the 1930s to make way for the extension of Gran Vía and later rebuilt in the 1940s as a low-rise redbrick affair. It's refreshing to find a market that's so firmly aimed at locals and with rock-bottom prices. Enter and you'll find yourself in a South American world of latin tunes, which reflects the majority of the stall holders, bar owners and locals of South American heritage – mainly Ecuadorian

Below and overleaf: *Multicultural Mercado de Los Mostenses*

and Peruvian – eating delicious food. A sweet start is the bakery by the entrance selling colourful and sugar-shiny Bolivian, Ecuadorian and Argentine specialties.

Although the Asian community is also represented – you can buy kimchi among the usual market food stalls, which reflect the local clientele's tastes, from greengrocers selling other Asian ingredients such as pak choi and Chinese cabbage to multiple grains, from dried beans and peas to soya beans and white quinoa. You'll also find fishmongers selling crab

and eel – fish you won't see in many other markets in Madrid – to butchers selling all manner of scary-looking animal parts, from pig's foot and tripe to cuajares de cerdo, giant pig's ears. If you're not here to buy – bad joke alert – offally-bad looking meat, head past the produce to the places where you can sit and imagine you are in a corner of Cuzco. Here, Peruvian food stalls include El Chiringuito Peruano, where a motherly cook serves comfort food such as papa rellenada, La Casa de los Mostenses dishes refreshing ceviche and Peruvian-Chinese fusion food at Lily, a Chifa (Chinese–Peruvian fusion) restaurant dishing crowd-pleasing noodle dishes and wonton soup.

All this and you can get your shoes reheeled while you're here. Note the street art decorating the walls, doors and stairs. The surrounding area is home to Chinese greengrocers and some down-to-earth tapas bars and restaurants including Peruvian.

Plaza de Los Mostenses, 1, 28015.

Mercado de Vallehermoso

All things to everyone, this ailing 1930s built Chamberí market had an inviting ruby-red facade but was fading on the inside with barely a handful of stalls until a makeover and injection of cash rejuvenated it. There's a permanent farmers' market on the ground floor, with small local businesses selling fair-priced foods, traditionally made or grown. Among the fresh produce, meat and seafood, you'll also find Spanish croquettes, Peruvian-inspired dishes, several small artisan beer stalls, one peddling lesser-known wines and cheese from La Mancha.

Calle Vallehermoso 36, 3628015, mercadovallehermoso.es

Mercado de Maravillas

Housed in a rationalist building, spanning an entire block, this aptly named Cuatro Caminos market (maravillas means wonders in Spanish) has the distinction of being the largest municipal marketplace in Europe, so expect to find pretty much everything among the 250 or so stalls. A strange mixture spanning fresh fruit and fish, Spanish charcuterie, handmade sausages, olives, spices, seasonal fruit, herbs, bull's testicles and sea urchins rubs shoulders with underwear, cleaning products, haberdashers and travel agencies. It's handily close to the Alvarado metro station, three miles north of the city centre, which keeps most tourists at bay. Hungry? Get your South American street food empanada fix at Venezuelan-run Pillalos and Peruvian ceviche from La Caleta de Dorita.

Calle de Bravo Murillo, 122, 28020, mercadomaravillas.eu

Mercado de Tirso de Molina

Like many of Madrid's municipal markets, this one built in 1932 by Luis Bellido, the same architect who designed the nearby Matadero Madrid cultural complex, has been brought back to life. Bullet marks left over from the Civil War can be seen on this brick market in the Puerta del Ángel neighbourhood not far from Madrid Río Park. Aside from the usual produce, there's craft beers to be drunk and Spanish charcuterie to be sampled among the Peruvian piscos and ceviches at Raza Inca, paellas cooked in front of you by top Valencian chefs at Paellamar and organic wine and artisan cheeses at La Desahuciada.

Calle de Doña Urraca 15, 28011, mercadotirsodemolina.es

Mercado de San Fernando

In multicultural Lavapiés, this much-loved market reflects its neighbourhood, home to natural wine bar, Bendito Vinos y Vinilos, where you can taste Spanish wines paired with bits of cheese and ham, and Mexican taco stands. It's also famed for its tortilla de patatas and locally made vermouth and craft beer. You can also find non-food items here, such as the volumes of books in the buy-by-weight La Casquería, clothing, arts, housewares and more.

Calle de Embajadores, 41, 28012.

Platea

In complete contrast to the more traditional markets, this has to be Madrid's most glamorous, naturally located in the Salamanca district. Originally a cinema, the five-floored theatrical design retains the red-curtained stages and balconies for watching the live music and shows while you sample food from all over the globe. Yes, there's Peruvian ceviche, yes there's Mexican tacos and yes there's a special tapas area, El Patio, where table service means diners can catch a show while nibbling on posh small bites. The head honchos are three Spanish chefs with a total of six Michelin stars between them.

Calle Goya 5–7, 28001, plateamadrid.com

Galerías Canalejas Food Hall

A few steps from Puerta del Sol, this posh food hall houses 13 restaurants and a gourmet zone (MAD Gourmet) with 20 speciality spaces. Here in the heart of Madrid, travel to Japan, Mexico, Italy, Galicia and more countries as you graze. What's not to like? Housed in a former bank, the original stained glass now decorating the main atrium, and the entrance features gold art deco-style detail and gold signage. With so much ostentation, you know there's going to be a Michelin-starred chef or two inside so close to designer stores such as Hermès and Zegna.

Calle de Alcalá, 12, 28014, galeriacanalejas.com

VEGAN & VEGETARIAN TAPAS

With its love of meat and fish, Madrid, and the whole of Spain, may not seem like an easy place for vegetarians and vegans to enjoy tapas. Enter traditional – and even contemporary – bars and you'll be faced with huge legs of ham hanging from the ceiling, or go to one of Madrid's many markets and you'll see all manner of fresh seafood on ice, not to mention porky nose-to-tail butchery, including pig's feet, ears and cheeks. For vegans, even the volume of cheese consumed is no doubt off-putting.

Vegetarian tapas is surprisingly easy to find in Madrid

However, finding vegetarian and even vegan food in Madrid is a little easier than you think. Spain doesn't really do vegetable side dishes, but enough of its traditional tapas dishes are naturally vegan, from patatas bravas to Padrón peppers, pan con tomate, salmorejo and gazpacho, while tortilla de patatas, huevos revueltos, croquetas and berenjenas are all vegetarian. Not to mention delicious. And now, as a growing number of restaurants are adding plant-based and vegetarian dishes to Madrid's multiplying tapas bars and restaurants, visitors with a conscience need never go hungry again.

It's all about knowing where to go and what to order.

Padrón peppers are packed full of vitamins

El Invernadero

You wouldn't expect to find a high-end vegetarian and vegan restaurant on Calle Ponzano in Chamberí, one of the most famous tapas streets in Madrid. Yet El Invernadero, meaning greenhouse in Spanish, is just that. Madrid-born chef and owner Rodrigo de la Calle creates what he calls 'green haute cuisine' – including gluten-free – so innovative and creative he won a Michelin star for his tasting menus a year after opening as well as a Green star for sustainability. He's worked with Martin Berasategui and Joël Robuchon, who've a few Michelin stars between them. While you can't really go wrong with any of the small plates created in the open kitchen, such as the artichoke hearts and purple sweet potatoes, the menus will change to reflect the seasonality of produce. Note some dishes contain meat protein for flavour so if you're strictly vegetarian or vegan, be sure to say and order the appropriate menu.

Calle Ponzano 85, 28003, elinvernaderorestaurante.com

Honest Greens

With four branches around the city at the time of going to press, you won't have to go far to find the nearest of these healthy-focused fast-food spots which are sprouting up around Spain, Portugal and the UK, where it's known simply as Hg. Created by three friends, most ingredients are organic and sourced from nearby suppliers but do note there is meat and fish on the menu, among the leafy greens. Choose from salads, grain bowls and protein platters that you can pair with plant-based sides. After a few of their sharing dishes such as raw beetroot ravioli with cashew 'ricotta', mint gremolata and caramelised walnuts or courgette carpaccio with beetroot tahini, toasted almonds, feta, mint and dill, you might be ready for some more tortilla de patatas.

Calle de Hortaleza,100, 28004, honestgreens.com

Mad Mad Vegan

Facing a sexy store for men's black leather posing pouches and other S&M-wear, among the gorgeous iron-clad balconies hung with rainbow flags, this slice of a bar and restaurant in Chueca always seems full. There's a sister restaurant in the city in Lavapiés, on the street of the same name, and another in Barcelona. The pun-loving chain features its 100% plant-based 'madnifiesto' online, which is to be a #chainbreaker (meaning multinationals). The menu divides easily into starters, where you'll find tapas-like bites from a dairy-free take on Venezuelan tequeños, deep fried worm-like pastry cases filled with sticks

of white cheese with a jam-like dipping sauce made from red fruits and another light green alioli; you can order three or six, and calamares rebozados, vegan squid battered in tempura, served with vegan mayo and lemon. Then there are the stars of the show, a variety of burgers made with plant-based patties with added cheese or chilli sauce. The brand's own beer is an artisan blonde ale made with organic malts. The slender space is set with high stools by the bar, and tables to the rear, with a blend of brick and stone walls and wooden beams.

Calle de Pelayo, 19, 28004, madmadvegan.com

Below and overleaf: *Tapas-like bites at Mad Vegan*

Secrets by Farga

While the name does sound more like a store selling sexy underwear than a health-food focused restaurant, that's exactly what this Spanish chain with branches in Madrid and Barcelona specialises in. The smart shop front and red awnings with the words 'Secrets by Farga' don't exactly scream 'we sell healthy vegan and vegetarian food' either, however, once in, welcoming young staff inhabit the bright diner-style space full of patterned cushions and prime colours, happy to help you choose your combination of protein and vegetables. The restaurants naturally thrive on Instagram with photos of filtered influencers kissing well-behaved poodles as they chow down on colourful vegan dishes or drink fresh combinations of juices full of chia seeds and ginger. It's an attractive easy-on-the-eye space to eat in or you can also take away tapas dishes such as potatoes 'casi bravas'

Below and overleaf: **Vegan and vegetarian tapas at Secrets by Farga**

or homestyle guacamole, which comes with tortilla chips in recyclable brown packaging tied with string.

Libertad 26, 28004, secretsbyfarga.com

Vega Alamo

Sister to Vega Luna in Malasaña, this Conde Duque vegan restaurant is tucked away behind the Plaza de España, a street up from the Mercado de los Mostenses. The characterful brick walls found in many a Madrid building are exposed, with the odd green planted trailing down, matching the tiles on the tables where you can try an international and fusion-filled menu made with organic ingredients along with local wines and beers. Many of the dishes are also gluten free. Popular tapas dishes include shitake mushroom croquettes with kimchi mayonnaise, ceviche made with setas (chanterelle mushrooms), edamame beans and served with yuca chips and jackfruit tacos on corn tortillas.

Calle del Álamo, 3, 28015, govega.es

Museo de La Empanada

The vegan and vegetarian dishes chalked up on the blackboard of this Colombian stall on the first floor of the massive Mercado de la Cebada in multicultural La Latina are served with a smile by the genial owner. They are also full of flavour, including arepas, large round corn flatbreads filled with cheese or vegan versions with cumin-flavoured kidney beans – great for protein – onions and tomato, served with a tiny pot of chilli sauce. Even meat and fish eaters pop by for these beauties.

Plaza de La Cebada, 28005.

Vegetarian Colombian classics at Museo de La Empanada at Mercado de la Cebada

8

HOTELS WITH TAPAS BARS

Often overlooked in favour of glitzier Barcelona, Madrid's showier coastal sibling, the capital of Spain, is equally, if not more, compelling with a personality and style all its own. Madrid has long mastered the art of the good life, and a love of it is more about understanding – and loving – the lifestyle lived out in its barrios and bars than gawping at its major monuments (although it has plenty of those, too). Spanish culture is built around good food and in a city with more bars than any other in the country – roughly 15,000 – where you can order a glass of chilled sangria and sample small amounts of quality food until the early hours, that all-important good life is easily found. Madrid has a unique food and drink scene because it is just that, in fact no city in Spain is like another. Despite the country's size, tapas, raciones and pinchos are firmly Spanish inventions, and you could be forgiven for thinking that you can only find the best of them in Madrid's many barrio bars and restaurants rather than in hotels.

However, when it comes to hotels, Madrid being Madrid, the city has every type of place to stay, from historic palaces to glamorous international brands now putting down roots here for the first time. Such hotels span those with in-house art galleries and rooftop spaces that show the sheer scale of the city, from the penned-in medieval centre to the greening around the edges, to those with in-house clubs and even bowling alleys. And this collection of existing and new hotels is home to restaurants and bars with tapas menus where, regardless of whether you're a guest or not, you can sample traditional or fusion-style dishes.

Here's a selection of hotels with tapas menus well worth trying.

Picos Pardos Sky Lounge by Martini, Bless Hotel Madrid

Salamanca, a smart neighbourhood of modern apartments and nineteenth-century mansions on broad streets, still has a down to earth feel, at least more so than the equivalent in cities such as London or New York. Here, the curved art deco exterior of the Bless Hotel on Calle de Velázquez is a welcoming sight – a large street-level door slides back to reveal a lounge-like lobby with spaces for taking afternoon tea, sinking down in squishy sofas, quaffing cocktails or dining late. So many colours and textures shouldn't work, but they do. You could be forgiven for not even realising it's a hotel at all – the reception is secreted in a far corner. You also probably wouldn't guess there's a resort-like space on the rooftop. To find it, head to the far side of the bar, take the tiny lift or seek out the original marble stairs that swirl upwards as far as they will take you.

What greets you as the lift door slides back is a sun-drenched, dream-like space divided between a small but appealing raised green-tiled swimming pool flanked by double Balinese daybeds and a restaurant, which keeps the hotel's love of colour going. Everything is pretty and decorative. You'll sit on chairs covered with paprika-coloured fabric or green with orange piping, eat with mottled silver cutlery surrounded by potted plants framing the glass balconies. The views are quite something, helped by Madrid being a city that has retained its

*Below and overleaf: **The glamorous Picos Pardos Sky Lounge at Bless Hotel Madrid***

low-lying horizon, so your gaze travels across the district's churches, ariels, tiled rooftops and domes.

Young staff help you choose what to eat, full of details on every ingredient, which ranges from tapas to larger dishes. The tapas are as good looking and colourful as the surroundings. Salmorejo, a southern Spanish dish made from sun ripened tomatoes, bread, extra virgin olive oil and garlic, is served in a blue and white ceramic bowl, where migas – tiny crumbs of crispy jamon and a quail's egg sit in the bottom before the waitress pours the chilled orange 'soup' over the top. In the summer heat, there's nothing more refreshing. A pair of sizable croquettes are as creamy as can be when broken open, revealing pieces of jamón inside the bechamel filling, topped with more. Just a handful of desserts include the torta de queso artesanal, a generous wedge of baked cheesecake that tastes like flan (crème caramel), at once fluffy, crunchy and super sweet. If you're not booked into one of the hotel's generously sized, eclectically styled rooms, after some sun, a cocktail and a full stomach, you'll wish you were.

Calle de Velázquez, 62, 28001, blesscollectionhotels.com

Dani Brasserie, Four Seasons Hotel Madrid

Despite opening as recently as 2020, which was slightly subdued by the pandemic, the Four Seasons Hotel Madrid seems as if it's been here for at least a century and in some ways it has. It's housed in the nineteenth-century Galerías Canalejas steps from Sol, a merger of seven buildings including several bank headquarters, a newspaper office and food hall

Below and overleaf: *Four Seasons Hotel Madrid and the rooftop Dani Brasserie*

and one of Madrid's most beautiful buildings, all art nouveau curves and cupolas. The two-storey lobby is a full-on fiesta of opulence, and some original features remain, such as the repurposed brass bannisters on the dramatical sweep of white marble staircase. Everything here is a bit 'extra' – the spa has four floors for yoga or massages and a 14-metre rooftop swimming pool glassed over for year-round use. Rooms layer rich, in all senses of the word, materials such as walnut and marble with Hermès bathroom products not far from the store selling the brand in the same street.

Entered from the street next door to the hotel, Dani Brasserie has the interior beauty you'd expect yet the benefit that you don't have to have the money to stay in the hotel to eat here. It's a well-oiled machine. Escorted to the lift, once on the top floor, the maitre'd greets you by name and escorts you into the restaurant. Even the hardest person to impress can't fail to be by the dreamy interiors, a mix of orange leather seating and upholstered green walls, which mirror the mass of plants everywhere you look. You'd be happy enough to be wined and dined inside, yet the terrace, which is on eye level with some of Madrid's most emblematic architecture, such as chariots and horses atop monumental buildings, offset by Madrid's ever-blue sky – is a charmer.

Colour is key here – staff wear bright green or orange trousers, which is probably just so that they match the potted palms and other foliage that are a large part of what's so appealing about the space. Also matching are the orange parasols with fancy gold fringing, big enough to cover four tables and provide shade in summer. But let's not forget the food. A selection of traditional tapas dishes is on the menu but naturally three Michelin-starred, Marbella-born chef Dani García 'who moved north from Andalucia' puts his own twist on the menu. Under the starters, crowd pleasers such as green gazpacho with tomate nitro (tomato prepared in liquid nitrogen) framed by a ring of baby shrimp tartare, are taken from his Leña Marbella restaurant. Even the jamón – acorn-fed Iberian ham in this case – is cut with precision into metro ticket-size thins fanned out across the plate. It isn't strictly tapas, but guacamole 'finished at the table' arrives in a large rustic mortar, topped with rice-crispy style tempura pieces, semi-dried tomato, edamame beans, sunflower seeds and served

with perfect tortilla chips. Despite the lavish care taken with all aspects of the hotel, this restaurant seems to be the showstopper.

Calle de Sevilla, 3, 28014, fourseasons.com/madrid

The Level Bar, The Generator

If the word 'hostel' brings to mind a charmless place with backpackers crammed into old iron beds in stuffy rooms with bare walls, think again. This converted 1930s petrol station is now a lively hostel well styled as a boutique hotel in one of the most central locations in the city, just off Gran Vía, a few steps from Santo Domingo metro station. As you'd expect, the majority of the guests do tend to be backpackers interspersed with families, couples and those here for work. Aside from multiple configurations of dorms, ranging from four- to eight-bed, including women only, king and twin rooms for one to two people feature painted panelling and studded bedheads in rich shades of green and orange with industrial touches from the wooden floors to the original concrete pillars striped with red paint.

Whichever room type you prefer, you can sit and enjoy tapas in the downstairs Level Bar, which brings 1980s diner-style vibes to an eclectically furnished space with red leather swivel stools, monochrome

Styled like a 1980s diner, the Generator's Level Bar dishes colourful tapas dishes and crunchy tacos

tiles and murals of Madrid sprawling up the walls. Vintage lampshades with tassels that are more grandma's living room than diner hang above the bar where you can stand and eat as in Madrid's more traditional bars. Or else find a spot to sit. The menu suits the space with a small selection of easy-to-eat tapas dishes such as rustic-style tortilla chips in shades of red and purple with small bowls of chunky guacamole and onion salsa and crunchy tacos. Order it all with a glass of fruity sangria made even prettier garnished with slices of fresh orange and physalis (a tiny round orange citrus fruit also called Cape gooseberry).

Up on the rooftop, Broken Shaker is an American import, creating an urban garden among the tiki-style bars and green and orange textiles. Youth-focused cocktails include the lemongrass and lime-juice-laced 'Bitch Don't Kill my Vibe.'

Calle de Silva, 1, Centro, 28013, staygenerator.com

El Oso Rojo, Radisson Red

At the Atocha station end of Calle de Atocha, in the middle of the so-called Art Triangle, the stretch between the Reina Sofía Museum, the Thyssen-Bornemisza and the Prado Museum, the Radisson Red is a colour-coded modern place to stay close to much of what draws travellers to Madrid. Once a sawmill in the 1800s, the decor bucks industrial references in favour of nods to the nearby museums, with murals inspired by Renaissance and Baroque-era art – rooms feature wall-sized murals of women in full skirts with clearly twenty-first-century numbered sports shirts on top.

The open-plan ground floor space encompasses a lounge area with art and coffee table books, a photo booth, Eneko Basque, Eneko Atxa's Michelin-starred restaurant and El Oso Rojo bar. The latter is naturally a red themed bar that's at once quite sexy and sociable with groups of chairs well placed between open shelves to divide the space, fluffy rugs and an illuminated red bar. Oso rojo means red bear in Spanish, you'll pass the red sculpture of a bear pawing a strawberry tree nodding to the famous original found in Puerta del Sol on your way in.

The small tapas menu lists enough options to mop up with a cocktail or two. The tomato salad is a thing of joy

El Oso Rojo bar at the Radisson Red

with purple-red plum-like tomatoes cut in quarters joined by white onion rings dressed with vinaigrette; an order of ham comes served on a wooden board with pickled green guindilla peppers, two types of ham and thick wedges of hard, slightly salty Manchego cheese. It's a good place to kick off a tapas trawl through the many bars and restaurants lining the streets around here.

Calle de Atocha, 123, 28012, radissonhotels.com

YOUnique Arts Club, Only YOU Boutique Hotel Madrid

This eclectically designed hotel, once a nineteenth-century palace, on the border of gay-friendly Chueca and traditional-meets-cool Salesas, is well located in an area that is one of Madrid's most charming. The surrounding streets are home to independent stores, bars and lovely architecture. One of the city's oldest theatres is opposite, the teeny Teatro Infanta Isabel is still showing plays and musicals in a jewel-box of a space lined with red seats lit by a chandelier. Inside the hotel, Catalan designer Lázaro Rosa-Violán has layered colour, patterns, textures and art to create a series of interconnecting public spaces, each pleasingly different from the other. Set against a backdrop of amazingly high ceilings and dark wooden beams, a classic

Mediterranean colour combination of blue and white is used throughout, from the pretty tiles covering a wall of lifts (the inside is lined with bookshelves) on the ground floor to the illuminated collections of ceramics in the breakfast room.

This is a hotel for enjoying food and drink in the many spaces designed for just that. Carved out of the palace's former library, the Padrino Cocktail Bar is a little like a museum, filled with old books left over from the original palace library and framed vintage posters. Here you can enjoy a pre-dinner vermouth and a selection of tapas spanning croquettes, patatas bravas and tripe. Alternatively, the YOUnique Arts Club is a stretch of spaces with iron columns, plants and design-led seating for fine dining on well-plated dishes such as carpaccio of wild sea bass with a creamy emulsion and a rich Spanish cheesecake you won't want to share. On Sundays, a brunch brings guests and no guests to the courtyard garden, lured as much by the DJ soundtrack as the menu of buttery pastries, charcuterie and main dishes such as eggs Benedict or barbecue ribs. If you're staying at the hotel, you'll enjoy rooms with a less lively decor than downstairs, but still smart with navy and mustard tones, and individuality coming from the differing shapes reflecting the building's heritage.

Calle Barquillo, 21, 28004, onlyyouhotels.com

Above and below: *Elegant dining spaces at the Only YOU Boutique Hotel Madrid*

La Terraza del Urban, Hotel Urban

Despite the smart doormen with long coats and tall top hats who welcome you through the glass doors into public areas rich with black stone, Champagne-coloured steel beams and Papua New Guinean statues – the basement gallery reveals the owners' private collection – there's something very relaxed about this hotel. Five minutes' walk from the Puerta del Sol, one of the busiest, tourist-and-busker-filled spaces in the city, it can feel more like a coastal resort than an urban hotel in the middle of Madrid.

A coastal resort that stands out with a glass and steel front, in contrast to the far older buildings in this area. As with all the Derby group hotels, large glass jars of sweet-shop-style sweets tempt you as you pass through reception. Two top Spanish chefs, Javier Sanz and Juan Sahuquillo, have won a Michelin star for the main Cebo restaurant and lead the menus throughout the hotel.

Rooms are what is often called masculine but that just means minimal, with lots of dark wood and leather, in shades of dark brown and black. They have windows that open, which is an attractive feature when you've had too

Below and opposite: Tapas, cocktails and the outdoor pool at the La Terraza del Urban at the Hotel Urban

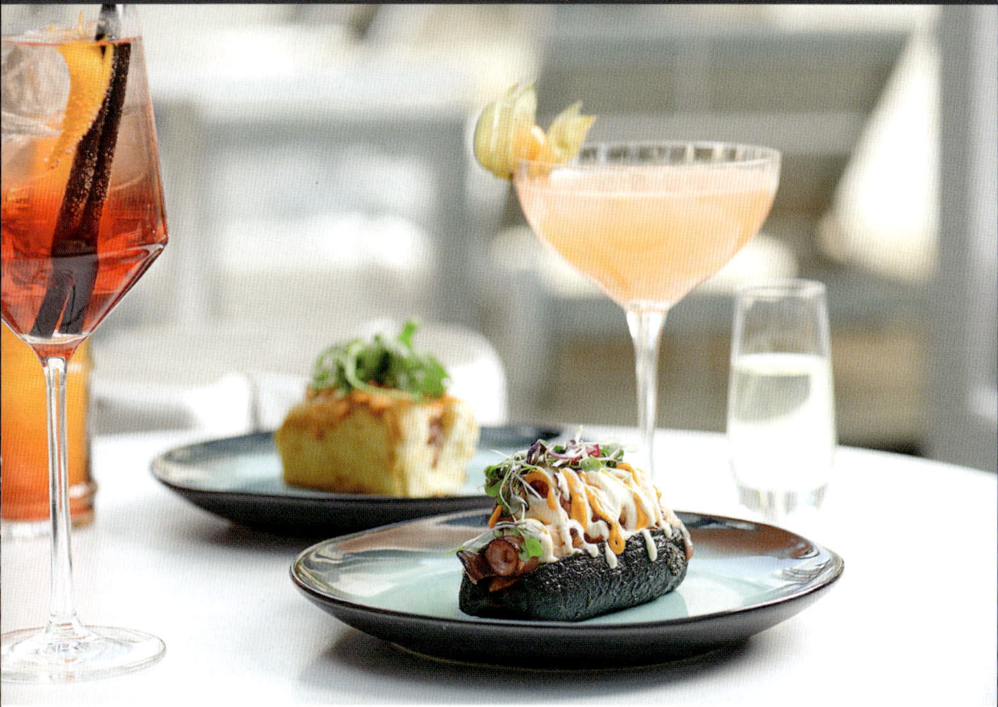

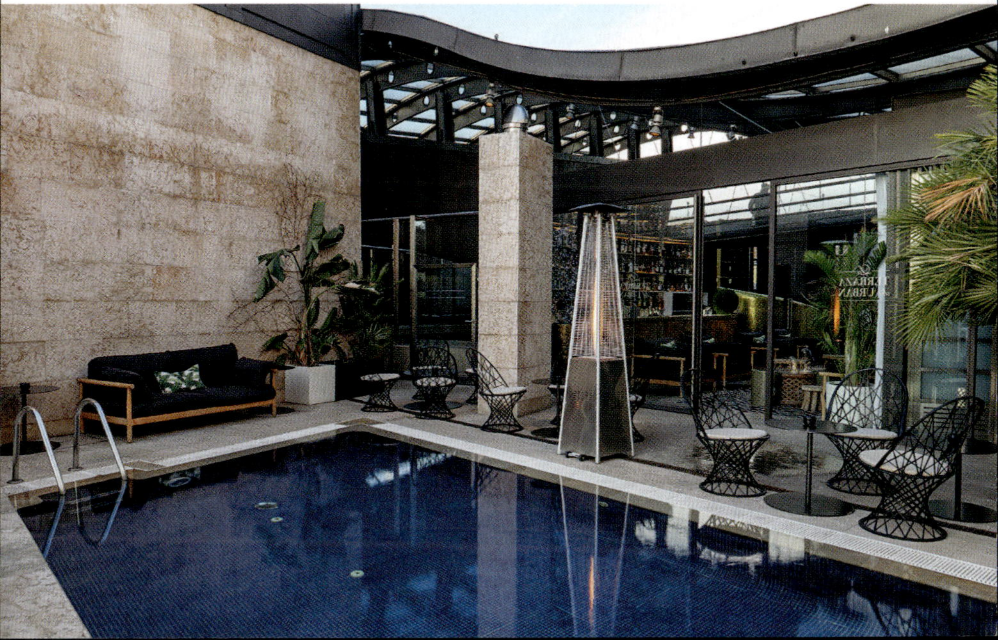

much air con. Bathrooms are a total contrast in white marble.

Up on the top floor, you'll find a glamorous gold mosaic tiled staircase on your way to the splash pool where buff men and families enjoy the small outside space entered via a glass-encased bar with wooden detail and black marble-topped tables. Here, tapas dishes are given the twist you'd expect from such a glamorous hotel overseen by Michelin-starred chefs, with a menu brimming with beautifully arranged tapas on pretty ceramic crockery. Sea bass ceviche is served on two chargrilled slices of lime with added crunch from toasted corn; Joselito ham and sheep's milk croquettes are small and perfectly formed and the octopus mini hotdog with homemade kimchi is a sight to behold.

On Fridays and Saturdays, DJs play until midnight, which is pretty tame for a late-night country like Spain, although the bar itself stays open until 2am. The staff throughout the hotel have a nice way with them, attentive yet easygoing.

Carrera de San Jerónimo, 34, 28014, hotelurban.com

Bar East 47, Hotel Villa Real

This refined hotel has a mixed style in terms of the eras the decor references, but it all somehow works, with a truly lovely team who extend a warm welcome. The hotel entrance faces the Spanish Parliament, on Plaza de las Cortes, actually a triangular square where skateboarders flip, and map-toting tourists pass by en route to queue up for hours to get into the Prado Museum. The large lobby is painted dark grey with pretty French-style sofas by the window to sit and drink a glass of lemon-infused water on or eat old-school sweets from the glass jars; a higher level houses a trio of Chesterfield sofas and potted palms with views across the square. It's almost worth your room not being ready to sit in this relaxing space.

And this being part of Derby Hotels, there's an unusual museum of restored Roman mosaics from Syria, dated between the second and sixth centuries, part of a catalogue of more than 100 found around the hotel's public spaces and rooms, collected by the well-travelled owner. Talking of which, rooms and suites veer on the traditional side, but they are comfortable and thoughtfully kitted out with lots of storage; some have sofa areas away from the bed space. Bathrooms are old-school green veined marble. On the rooftop there's a contemporary seasonal pool, bar and sunbathing area.

From a completely different era, but keeping an art connection, the ground floor East 47 bar is named after Andy Warhol's studio on 47th Street on New York's East Side. Pop

Above, below and overleaf: *Colourful tapas dishes at East 47 bar at Villa Real*

art prints of Marilyn Monroe line the back wall, where you can sit on banquettes – or the terrace on the square (actually a triangle) trying the tapas menu. Tapas staples are given a special touch and prettily presented, from smoked sardines with apple and basil to crunchy fried pork belly strips with guacamole to a beautiful pink tomato salad, with a large beefy slice of pinky-red tomato dressed with mango, avocado and black olives. Not forgetting good old jamón ibérico.

Plaza de las Cortes 10, 28014, hotelvillareal.com

Michelin-Starred Tapas in Hotels

Some highly conceptual tapas bars are housed in hotels. Some are by Michelin starred stars of the Spanish food scene including chefs such as Ramón Freixa, Paco Roncero and Dabiz Muñoz, who operate flagship restaurants in Madrid.

There are honestly too many Michelin-starred restaurants in Madrid to keep track of but here's a few to consider if you like your tapas high end.

Take **Estado Puro**, a tapas bar from two-Michelin-starred chef Paco Roncero, one of Spain's molecular gastronomists who once worked in El Bulli restaurant.

He creates avant garde tapas and experimental Spanish dishes that riff on the traditional such as alioli potatoes presented like a work of cubist art and a club sandwich served in a surrealist spiral. The design-led decor includes an arched gold ceiling, OTT light fixtures and kitsch murals and you can find it in the NH Collection Madrid Paseo del Prado. If you've never tried Michelin-star croquettes made from oxtail and bulls' tail, and have deep pockets, book a table here.

Plaza Cánovas del Castillo 4, 28014, tapasenestadopuro.com.

Another is Ricardo Sanz's Wellington in the Hotel Wellington in Salamanca. Here, Ricardo and his team produce clever things by mixing sushi and sashimi with Mediterranean influences in an open kitchen. The restaurant was awarded a Michelin star for the signature dishes, including huevos rotos with the eggs served with fingers of Canary Island potatoes instead of the usual chips and bluefin tuna instead of ham.

Calle de Velázquez, 6, 28001, gruporicardosanz.com

DiverXO, the only three Michelin-starred restaurant in Madrid, is currently housed – it moves around – in the NH Collection Madrid Eurobuilding in Paseo de la Castellana. Creative chef Dabiz Muñoz's fantastical dishes are served on canvases and among the

fantastical circus-like surroundings, with flying pigs wearing tutus on walls. Diners sample the fittingly named flying pig's menu, which combines local ingredients with those from further afield.

NH Collection Madrid Eurobuilding, Calle del Padre Damián, 23, 28036, diverxo.com

If pigs could fly: fantastical food and interiors at DiverXO

TAPAS TOURS

The best – and some might argue the only – way to eat tapas is to take your time moving from bar to bar, choosing each for its particular food or drink speciality. Or perhaps for its location. Most bars have a range of tapas displayed under glass on their counters or written on their blackboard, menu board or menu, although many are known for certain dishes so why would you order anything else? You'll start in one place known for its pimientos de Padrón, moving on to a temple to pulpo de Gallega then another for its jamón serrano. Of course, drinking and eating tapas go hand in hand,

The Habsburg-designed Plaza de Mayor is a grand square with a storied history close to dozens of tapas bars

you can't really have one without the other, which is at the root of why the Spanish aren't falling down drunk in bars. So, you might also choose a bar by its reputation for vermouth on tap or draft beer.

To get a feel for Madrid, you need to branch out from the obvious sights and experience the different vibes of its various barrios. Tapas tours are a good way for someone not familiar with Madrid to experience a bunch of bars in one hit, guided by a plugged in and usually charismatic local who knows what to order and where. Letting someone else lead while you follow can lead to one of the best days of your trip and that sought-after cliche – immersion in local life. It's in the markets and tapas bars where you'll really eat like a local, and most tours weave around them both. You'll meet generations of stall holders or bar staff and learn what the most popular – and sometimes unpalatable – tapas dishes are (yes, we're talking snails and tripe). The stories behind each dish, history of each bar and the areas they are found in, will all be regaled and revealed on a guided tour.

Official tapas tours can be private, or group, the latter a good option for solo travellers or those of us that like socialising while away. Tapas tours also range in price, from free itineraries to lengthy day-long affairs with lots of stops for a wide variety of food and wine. It's also useful if your Spanish is non-existent or not that good, so you end up with what you want to order and not something entirely different.

Of course, armed with this book – or not – you may prefer just to wander where you like, when you like. That can be a more spontaneous experience with no time limitations or rules to stick to. Where you go is entirely up to you, but the best time is probably in the evening, when the city comes to life. Whether you're a tourist or a local, you'll all be on some kind of tapas tour as you hop from bar-to-bar sampling dishes and drinks. Madrid is a very walkable city, and streets are surprisingly safe, even in the early hours of the morning.

ToursByLocals

ToursByLocals is an international outfit with tours across the globe, always led by firmly local guides who connect with guests via the website. Madrid tours include those with a strong focus on wine, some mixing history with tapas and wine, others focus on the city's many famous museums or even pick you up in a chauffeured vehicle. Whichever tapas-based tour you pick, you'll stop at around four bars or restaurants while you get a generous portion of history on the side. Tours are personalised, so if you want more of something and less of another, that's no problem. You'll end the tour full of food, naturally, but also of fascinating facts that will add to your experience of Madrid and that you can trot out to impress your friends and family.

As history-buff Kwame whisked me around the central La Latina and Las Austrias districts, he pointed out churches such as the multi-tiered, domed – the fourth largest in Europe – Royal Basilica of Saint Francis the Great, home to an early work by Goya near the Mercado de Cebada. Also, the forensic-level history to be found detailed in metal plaques on circular benches in the Plaza de Mayor such as the three-day fire in 1790 (who else would know this level of information?). We ate our way around some of Madrid's many restaurants specialising in one dish, sampling chorizo-stuffed mushrooms at the cave-like Mesón del Champiñón and Kwame graciously accepted my firm 'no' at his smiling suggestion I ate the famous snails swimming in the secret house sauce at Los Caracoles. I didn't need nudging to down a strawberry-infused shot – a chupito – in an edible chocolate-lined wafer cup at El Madroño, nor salty, some-hot, some-not Padrón peppers and crispy potatoes in Bar Cruz. As we walked around the city streets, we discussed the merits of various bars we didn't have time to stop at, so that another time, I could.

toursbylocals.com

Kirker Holidays/Devour Tours

Kirker Holidays specialise in tailor-made short breaks to a variety of European cities and the Kirker Concierge arranges private guided tours, opera and concert tickets and restaurant recommendations. For their Madrid customers, the company is working with Devour Tours, who focus on family-run venues and mix up their itineraries to vary the route and the bars and restaurants they include. Guides such as Dani, a professional chef, take a lot of trouble to explain how the tour will go, getting guests to engage with him and each other, which may seem cringey at first, but it works. By the end of a four-hour tour, my group was mixing nicely, in-jokes were bandied about while Dani talked us through each dish and drink we consumed. We weaved through the city stopping at four places – all of them reviewed in this book – starting at Taberna Real for jamón and toasted almonds with the sweet vermouth on tap the former Royal staff quarters is known for. We walk through the Royal Palace gardens, seeking shade by the greenery, as we learn about King Ferdinand and Queen Isabella, second cousins who ruled Spain in the fifteenth century. We tried not to spill mushroom juice down our chins at Mesón del Champiñón before sipping sweet red wine and garlic prawns at La Casa del Abuelo. The time passed quickly,

Above: *Chorizo-stuffed mushrooms at the cave-like Mesón del Champiñón*

Below: *Devour Tours focus on family-run venues*

with our final meal at Los Galayos, a restaurant housed in a creaky old seventeenth-century building with a carved wooden bar and dark beams. Tortilla de patatas, black-pudding-like morcilla with a side of ratatouille-like pisto and good red and white wines (Rioja and Albariño). Salud!

kirkerholidays.com; devourtours.com

A selection of other tapas tours to try...

The guides leading **Insiders Travel** private tapas tours include artists, flamenco dancers and jazz musicians, and aim to connect people, so they feel part of things, teaching guests cultural dos and don'ts, including the vital how to order – by elbowing your way to the front of the bar. Owned by the González family, El Sobrino de Botín – which you may now know is the oldest restaurant in Madrid – exclusively works with Insider Travel to create guided exclusive tours through the atmospheric old space with four dining rooms, the medieval cellar and series of tunnels before a seven-dish dinner including tapas and wine.

Insiders Travel tapas bar tours (Insiders Travel, Kelly Hurd)

Roast suckling pig at El Sobrino de Botín (Insiders Travel by Kelly Hurd)

Dishing tapas since 1906, **La Casa del Abuelo** is one of a family-run collection of bars and restaurants in the centre of Madrid, who also organise tapas tours, which naturally take in some of their legendary bars. The oldest one is in Calle Victoria, with two more across the street. Their clutch of tapas tours includes one focused on the Mercado de la Paz in Salamanca, home to the most famous tortilla de patatas in Madrid and one around the Barrio de las Letras literary quarter.

lacasadelabuelo.es

Withlocals tours connect travellers and guides across an international platform. The Madrid tours include vegetarian options, with tailor made tours taking in three 'bites and drinks in Lavapiés to 10 tastings with stops at historical spots around the centre of Madrid.

withlocals.com

Get stuck into a heady world of tapas in the multicultural Lavapiés neighbourhood with the **Tapapiés tapas festival** each October. It's a ready-made tapas tour with around 100 bars, restaurants and markets plotted on a numbered map. It's inclusive and affordable with tapas dishes for €3.50 per tapa including a bottle of beer, surrounded by bands and street parades. If you fall in love with a particular dish, you can vote for it at the end.

enlavapies.com

ACKNOWLEDGEMENTS

I owe a lot of thanks to a lot of people, many who trawled the streets of Madrid with me eating a lot of tapas along the way. While that's not that hard, my sisters Maria and Victoria Fernández, friends Zena Alli, Alicia Deza and Andrea Cumberbatch put the hours in. Alicia, Victoria, Maria and Cati Fernández also helped with the authenticity of family stories and Spanish traditions, which Megan Fernández was also a part of. Big thanks to Rosa Sibaja for her support and introduction to her cousin Maria Gonzalez de la Fuente; and to my daughter Maya for her encouragement and feedback; Kate Simon, who helped organise my schedule and chapters; Natasha Troy who fed my two cats so I could flit back and forth to Madrid for six months. Thanks also to the chefs who took time out of busy kitchens to share their recipes and recommendations, the Spanish Tourist Office and all the PRs who helped me organise stays, Devour Tours, Kirker and Joanna and Heather at Insider Tours who helped with photos (the bane of my life).

In writing about something so sociable and such a part of Spain's strong culture, I may have become a little boring; now I can go back to eating and drinking without taking notes. Even the sometimes grumpy barmen of Madrid deserve thanks for serving the food and drink that make up the core chapters of this book.

And thank you, Dad, because without you I probably wouldn't have become so fascinated with tapas and Madrid.

BIBLIOGRAPHY

Krishna, Vamsi, *Muslim Walls of Madrid* (Atlas Obscura, https://www.atlasobscura.com)

The perfect combination for hitting upon the best suckling pig (https://botin.es)

Devour Tours (https://devourtours.com)

C. Fanjul, Sergio, *Madrid's hungry years* (El País English, https://english.elpais.com)

ES Madrid (https://www.esmadrid.com)

Generator Madrid, (https://staygenerator.com/hostels/madrid?lang=en-GB)

Lonely Planet, *Madrid, Spain* (https://www.lonelyplanet.com/spain/madrid)

Rough Guide to Spain (Rough Guides, London, 2009)